D1187180

SPANISH COOKING

ELIZABETH CASS

Spanish Cooking

ANDRE DEUTSCH
for
THE COOKERY BOOK CLUB

This edition published 1968 by
The Cookery Book Club
9 Grape Street, London, W.C.2
for sale only to its members.

Originally published 1957 by
Andre Deutsch Limited
Second impression 1968

Printed in Great Britain by
Lowe & Brydone (Printers) Ltd.,
London

CONTENTS

CONTENTS

INTRODUCTION

★

SOME HISTORICAL FACTS

REGIONS AND RECOMMENDED DISHES

HERBS AND FLAVOURINGS

SOME TYPES OF SPANISH SAUSAGES

WINES AND LIQUEURS

SPANISH CHEESES

ACKNOWLEDGEMENTS TO RESTAURANTS

Despuès de buen comer, ni libro ni mujer.
After a good meal, neither a book nor a woman.

This book is intended to give a general idea of the principles of Spanish cooking. With the exception of the large tome of the Condesa Pardo Bazán, which is a comprehensive manual giving international cookery, there are really no good Spanish cookery books. The recipes generally state that such and such a thing is used, but no exact quantities are given. This may be useful to refresh the memory of an experienced cook but not to initiate a beginner.

Spain is rich in recipes but most of them have been handed down by word of mouth from one generation to another, and in the course of time they have become considerably modified; not only does one find that a recipe having the same name varies considerably in the different towns of Spain but also from house to house, and it is extremely difficult to write some of these recipes in an accurate form as one finds that the local cooks, although they can make the dishes, cannot give exact quantities. In fact, every one uses his imagination and gives his own individual touches according to taste. One has to take these recipes down verbally and everyone is delightfully vague about details. This failing, alas, is not exclusively Spanish as many other cooks who know how to cook a dish themselves find it difficult to pass on a recipe to others.

The natural resources of Spain are abundant but entirely different from those which are found in England. One must remember that the average Spaniard would despise English cooking exceedingly, as certainly many English people would dislike Spanish cooking all day and every day.

Olive oil, in the vast majority of Spanish dishes, takes the place of butter, and fish, chicken and eggs are often preferred to meat. There are two distinct kitchens in Spain, one that of the de luxe hotel which has very similar food—apart from a few national dishes—to a de luxe hotel in any other country, and the other, the regional cooking which one finds in small restaurants all over Spain (some excellent and some extremely bad), and also in Spanish houses, if one is lucky enough to be invited. One should not come away with the impression that Spanish cooking is greasy. Greasy cooking is bad cooking anywhere and actually oil is the most easily digestible fat for the human being and is far better than mutton or pork fat for frying. It does not leave a residue on the food, as, for example, one finds on potatoes fried in fat. These, when they get cold, usually have a distinct layer of grease on them however carefully one has strained the potatoes, whereas when they are cooked in oil this does not occur.

It must also be realized that ovens in many cases do not exist and the cooking is done on a charcoal or wood fire. One therefore finds a lot of fried food and stews, which are more common than roasts for which an oven is essential.

The long lunch hour in Spain gives one time to appreciate one's food, but don't think that Spaniards work shorter hours. Offices and shops open later in the afternoon, they work later in consequence and often for longer hours than the English.

It is very difficult to say what a typical Spanish midday meal is, but usually one starts with entremeses (hors-d'œuvre) or in the south perhaps a few tapas, which are modified hors-d'œuvre in the form of small snacks taken with drinks before a meal, i.e. olives, almonds, pieces of fried fish or anchovies (fresh or tinned), pieces of meat, cheese, etc. This is then probably followed by a soup and a dish of fish or eggs with rice, then meat or chicken and finally fruit because it is not often in Spain that one has a sweet course. The sweets are pastries and usually only eaten on special occasions. Breakfast varies from a cup of coffee to the traditional chocolate accompanied by a glass of milk and churros. Churros are made from a dough rather like the mixture we use for doughnuts, which is pulled out into long thin strips and then fried and rolled in sugar. Tea is a meal which does not exist in Spain, and supper, which can be served at any time from eight until midnight, usually after 9 pm, is a lighter edition of lunch.

SOME HISTORICAL FACTS

Spain has a variety of dishes which are quite unknown to the majority of people outside Spain, and sometimes outside their own region. A large number of these traditional dishes have been taken by France at various times and refined and altered, but can still be recognized by their names in the books of cookery experts such as Escoffier; for example, Pheasant à l'Alcantare and various dishes 'à l'Andalouse', which usually contain both red peppers and tomatoes.

Original Spanish dishes have been modified and changed by invaders and also by people who founded colonies and then came back to Spain bringing traditional dishes of other countries with them. The Romans brought many such dishes and introduced garlic and oil to the Spaniards. The Celtic influence found in the north of Spain and in Galicia is responsible for the use of animal fat instead of oil for frying and for the absence of garlic. The Arab invasion gave Spain new methods of cooking, for the Arabs brought with them hitherto unknown spices from Persia and India; they also brought lemons, oranges and grapefruit—oranges were then called 'the apples of Persia' and these gave rise to the tale of the 'golden apples' in the Gardens of the Hesperides. At a later date the sweet orange from China was introduced by the Portuguese.

Amongst the spices brought by the Arabs were saffron, nutmeg and black pepper, and above all they introduced sugar cane and sugar. During the occupation of Spain Arab cooking was more civilized than that of the rest of Europe and it spread to France and up the Mediterranean to Italy and even farther north to Flanders and Germany. It was after the discovery of America that various new elements were introduced into civilized cooking, amongst them the potato, the tomato, chillies, red and green peppers, also cocoa and chocolate. It is said that until the middle of the seventeenth century chocolate was not known in France, but the Spanish Infanta, Maria Teresa of Austria—when she married Louis XIV—came to the Court in Versailles with a maid who used to make chocolate for her to drink, of which she was very fond; but it was Anne of Austria who first introduced Spanish dishes to the Royal Court. Spanish cooking, however, was usually looked down upon by the French who considered it unrefined. The Spaniards claim that it was they who invented flaky pastry in 1611 and that it was later adopted by France. The Valencian Ali-oli was the original of the French Aioli; the first recipe was said to exist in Spain in 1024 and it was later introduced into Provence.

Tomatoes were first introduced into Spain one hundred years before they were introduced into France. Spain was probably responsible for the first Pot au Feu, i.e. the Spanish Olla Podrida. The original Spanish Tortilla gave birth to the so-called French omelette and was claimed to have been made in 1637 by a cook of Philip IV and introduced into the Court of Louis XIV by that same Spanish maid of Maria Teresa of Austria.

In those days the Spaniards were known to have an abundance of everything and their meals had many courses; for example, Philip and Isabel would give banquets at which 500 dishes were served, showing great diversity of fish, meat, birds, etc.

It was during the eighteenth and nineteenth centuries that many recipes were imported from Spain into France. In 1757 the Duke of Richelieu won the battle of Mahon in Minorca. To celebrate this his cook modified the Ali-oli and called it Mahonese (mayonnaise), which was later imported into France.

During the invasion of Napoleon many dishes were imported into France by French officers. In the convents and monasteries were manuscripts of recipes, some of the most famous being from the monastery at Alcántara. The marzipan of the monastery of Escorial was famous, as were many of the other sweets and pastries. At a later date the Empress Eugénie also imported some of the best Spanish cooking into the French Court.

REGIONS AND RECOMMENDED DISHES

For the benefit of those who are thinking of visiting Spain I have taken the ancient divisions of the country and have given the names of the provinces in each division, with a brief description of the game, meat, fish, vegetables, etc., and some of the special dishes to be found there.

ANDALUSIA

Provinces: Sevilla, Huelva, Cadíz, Málaga, Granada, Jaén, Almería, Córdoba.

The eight provinces of Andalusia have distinctive cooking. Many cookery books contain recipes for dishes 'l'Andalouse'.

These are usually flavoured with tomatoes and red peppers and cooked in oil. This, however, is only a small part of the cooking of Andalusia, much of which resembles the cooking of Provence. Each province has its own specialities, although there is a certain similarity between them. But in spite of the excellent recipes in these provinces there are few good cooks—the standard of cooking in the south of Spain is often bad. And abundance of natural resources goes hand in hand with poor cultivation and hard soil.

All down the coast one finds innumerable fish, of which the foreigner is often ignorant. Oranges, lemons, figs, peaches, pears, grapes, custard apples, prickly pears, almonds and pomegranates, loquats and melons of all descriptions are to be found in their seasons. It is from Andalusia, from the little town of Jerez-de-la-Frontera, that the world is supplied with sherry. There we find the famous Bodegas, many of which are English owned or have English partners, and if one goes to a Bodega one finds that they are only too pleased to show visitors how sherry is produced. At the Bodega of Williams & Humbert with its famous green lawn and its peacock, Mr Guy Williams' son-in-law, one of the young Domecqs—who speaks perfect English—is always a genial host. At the large, and among the oldest, Bodega of Palomina and Vergara, the English manager, Mr Bullman, always makes one welcome. Then there are the famous old firms of Domecq and Gonzalez Byass, who are more than hospitable to strangers in Jerez, but one must have a strong head to carry one through the day. The Hotel Los Cisness in Jerez has a lovely old courtyard and bar, and good cooking. A speciality of Jerez is Calderete de Jerez (a lamb stew), and brandy is found there as well as sherry.

SEVILLE. In Seville it is well worth asking for 'Huevos a la

Flamenca', a dish with fried eggs on top of peas, beans, onions, pimientos and little chorizos (garlic sausages). Even if you are not fond of tripe, the Menudo Gitana is a revelation. Instead of being the tough leathery article one often finds in England, it is deliciously soft and excellently flavoured. Veal a la Sevillana is another popular dish.

Seville has also given its name to Pato a la Sevillana, a duck dish which Londoners may know from Martinez, the Spanish restaurant in Swallow Street.

In the city of Antequera, and in Rhonda, they make little biscuits such as polvorones, mantecados, alfajores and moste-chones. They are rather dry but good eaten with sherry. From one of the gourds called sidra, delicious jam is made which has the romantic name of 'Cabello de Angel'—angel's hair—be-cause, when cooked, the fine strands look like golden hairs.

Dishes to ask for

HUELVA. This province produces delicious hams and pork. All round the coast one finds sardines, red, brown and grey bream, the deep-sea bream called pargo, skate, whiting, the little almejas or cockles, tunny fish, deep-sea prawns, sword-fish, squids and cuttlefish.

In this province one can eat Pargo Encebollado (which is
sea bream cooked with tomato and onion sauce), little cockles
cooked with rice, fish soups, tunny fish or bonito cooked with
tomatoes, langostinas (Dublin Bay prawns) cooked with sauce,
squids cooked with beans and swordfish in many forms.

Dishes to ask for

CADIZ. As we go down the coast from Seville we come to
the Province of Cadíz. It is from this region that most of the
sherry-type wines come. The vegetables and fruit here include
delicious globe artichokes, tomatoes, red and green peppers,
melons, gourds and oranges. There are also plenty of chickens
and ducks. An especially delicious grey mullet is fished in the
Bay of Cadíz. Also in Cadíz and down this coast we get a
variety of shellfish, crab, lobsters, etc, and one can also eat a
small shellfish resembling an oyster, called ostión, which cannot, however, be eaten raw.

Dishes to ask for

MALAGA. In the Province of Málaga one can sit and eat chanquetes, which resemble English whitebait, served fried and eaten as tapas with one's sherry. Again fresh fish such as 'rape', bass, red mullet, hake or ling and various shellfish are found in abundance.

Málaga itself produces a sweet wine, rather heavy and too sweet for our English taste, and also a beer. All over this region the most beautiful grapes are grown and also sugar cane, figs, oranges, tomatoes, almonds and pomegranates.

The Café Alegrías gives one excellent chanquetes. Arroz a la Marinera, the rice dish containing a variety of shellfish, is typical of the local cooking. One of the most famous dishes in Málaga is a soup which is made with grapes or melon, which is served ice cold in the summer and is delicious. This is called Sopa de Ajo Blanco con Uvas or, more rarely, Sopa de Ajo Blanco con Melón.

Also famous, not only in Málaga but all along the coast, is another cold soup, which, if properly made, is most delicious on a hot day, besides being extremely nourishing; this is Gazpacho. It varies from home to home as there is no fixed recipe and the quantities of the ingredients vary as you like but the essentials are always the same, i.e. tomatoes, cucumber, garlic, onions, oil, vinegar, breadcrumbs. Málaga also has a factory for making its own pasta such as spaghetti, vermicelli and macaroni. Recipes for Fideos a la Malagueña (Spaghetti à la Malagueña) will be found on pp. 265-6. The sweet potato which comes from Málaga is particularly good and is served either as a vegetable or as a sweet.

Dishes to ask for

GRANADA. From the Province of Granada come very good broad beans, peas and French beans, spinach and silver beet. There is also a ham known as Jamon de Trévelez.

Dishes to ask for

JAEN. In Jaén we again find spinach and vegetables, and in their season luscious cherries and apples. From this province come the following recipes:

Meat
Sauce

ALMERIA. In the Province of Almeria the most succulent grapes are grown.

A good dish to ask for is: *Page*

CORDOBA. This is a fertile province with good agriculture and plenty of lamb, mutton, etc. Montilla and Los Morillas produce good local wine. Anis (aguardiente) is made in Rute, and Monturo has excellent olives for the production of olive oil. Honey, chick-peas and quinces, which are used for quince jelly and quince cheese, abound.

Dishes to ask for

VALENCIA

Provinces: Valencia, Alicante, Castellon de la Plana

ALICANTE. The ali-oli probably originated in Alicante. It was known as early as the tenth century and was probably imported by the Romans and may be the 'moretum' mentioned in Virgil. It is used extensively to accompany grills, roasts, etc, of meat, fish and game.

Dishes to ask for

VALENCIA. This is a very fruitful district producing rice and sugar, oranges, lemons, grapefruit, etc. It is the home of the most famous rice dishes. Paella Valenciana, containing chicken, meat, crayfish, mussels and hake, is a marvellous dish; the name paella is taken from the pan in which it is cooked.

Mostachones: little Cakes eaten at christenings, wed-
dings, and Corpus Christi
Cuajada: Junket   290
Wine
Valencia produces an excellent Vino Tinto Corriente
(locally produced Red Wine in barrels).

MURCIA

Provinces: Murcia, Albacete

Here begins the cooking of the east of Spain. The mujol (a
form of mullet) is famous and so also are the deep-sea prawns.
Tomatoes and pimientos are prevalent in the cooking, and
saffron is a herb which is cultivated in this region.

Dishes to ask for

Soup   *Page*
Potaje Murciana: Soup with Red Beans, French Beans
and Rice
Eggs
Tortilla Murciana: Omelette with Tomatoes and
Pimientos   84
Vegetables
Menestra de Legumbres Frescas: a mixed Vegetable
Dish   263

CATALUNIA

Provinces: Barcelona, Gerona, Lérida, Tarragon

Catalunian cooking is quite distinctive and shows both French
and Italian influences. Bouillabaisse and various other fish
stews and soups are to be found here.

Dishes to ask for

  Tarragona produces a heavy port-like red wine of this name.

ARAGON

Provinces: Zaragoza, Huesca, Teruel.

This region has an excellent cuisine. Lamb and chicken are good. Fruits such as greengages, peaches, pears, apples and apricots, cherries and strawberries appear in their season.

ZARAGOZA. Zaragoza has a name for good cooking.

Dishes to ask for

They have their own local wine and mulled claret for
Christmas-time.

NAVARRE

There is only one province of Navarre and the cooking is very
similar to that of Aragón and is also allied to that of France.

There are the most succulent lambs for the table and trout abounds in the river. There is good cheese from Roncal and the wines of Tudela and of Peralta to accompany the meat. Chocolate is used to thicken the sauce of the local partridge, and very good it is too.

THE BASQUE COUNTRY

Provinces: Viscaya (capital Bilbao), Alava (capital Vitoria), Guipuzcoa (capital San Sebastian).

The Basque country has a number of dishes which are famous. The one which is most commonly known to tourists is Bacalao a la Vizcaína. But with the profusion of fresh fish such as hake, eels, inkfish, bream, sardines, skate, bonito, etc., there are, as one would expect, many other good fish recipes. Pork and lamb are good in this region, as they are in most of the north of Spain.

Dishes to ask for

LEON

Provinces: León, Palencia, Salamanca, Valladolid, Zamora.

There are various famous recipes in this region bearing the names 'a la Leonesa' or 'a la Berciana', or associated with the name of Astorga, which is famed both in Spain and South America for its little cakes and biscuits.

It is a rich country with fertile grazing land, and rivers with an abundance of trout and eels. There is also excellent fruit and vegetables. Chocolate is one of the favourite drinks in this region, and it is also used in the cooking of partridge, etc.

Dishes to ask for

GALICIA

Provinces: Coruña, Lugo, Orense, Pontevedra.

The Galicians are proud of their kitchen and rightly so. They have a fertile land and delight in good food. Both river and sea fish is varied and good; the best oysters in Madrid come from Galicia and there are good cockles, eels, octopus and inkfish, etc. The land is good for the production of fruit and the feeding of animals. Chestnuts are abundant and excellent marrons glacés are made. Pork, ham and sausages are plentiful.

Dishes to ask for

Jamon: Ham
Cachelos: a Dish of Vegetables and Ham
Lacon con Grelos: Dried Ham and Cabbage   197
Rice
Arroz con Mejillones: Rice with Mussels   162
Egg Dish
Huevos con Mariscos: Eggs with a form of Small
    Scallop   92
Sweets
Marrons Glacés
Amoados: Biscuits made with Oatmeal
Torta de Almendras: Almond Tart
Torrija   288
Carne de Membrillo: Quince Cheese
Cabello de Angel: Pumpkin Jam   291
Wines
The following, which are table wines, red and white, come
from the Province of *Orense*:

Ribeiro
Valdeorras
Tres Rios
Arnoya
Untes ('En Untes bebe y no preguntes' they say locally: 'In
    Untes drink and don't ask questions.')
Trasalba
Carballino ('Para carne, pan y vinoo Carballiño': 'To put on
    weight: bread and wine, or Carballino'—another local
    saying.)

The following come from the Province of *Pontevedra*:

Ramollasa

Condado
Vino Espumoso (like sweet Champagne).

Cheeses
The Province of *Galicia* produces the following:

Queso del Cebrero
Queso de San Simon
Queso de San Pantaleon
Queso de Santiago
Queso de Guimarey ('Para mulas, Monterroso, Para
   ladrones, la curia, Para quesos, Guimarey.' This is a local
   verse meaning that you should go to Monterroso to find
   mules, to the police court to find thieves and to Guimarey
   to find cheeses.)

ASTURIAS

Province: Oviedo

It was upon the food of this Province that the foundation of
South American cookery was laid. It is similar to that of
Galicia, Brittany and Normandy. The tourist will find a
number of famous dishes, amongst which is Fabada.

Apples are good and plentiful both for eating and for making
cider. The chestnut is also excellent in this region and there is
a festival where engaged couples (novios) eat chestnuts together.

Dishes to ask for

Soup	*Page*
Sopa de Coles a la Asturiana: Cabbage Soup	66
Vegetables	
Fabada Asturiana: Bean Soup	254

'El cantelo era bueno	'The cantelo was good
y dejara memoria.	and will be remembered.
No dejeis sin parte	Don't leave the bride
a la Señora novia.'	without a piece.'

LOCAL VERSE

CASTILLA LA NUEVA

Provinces: Madrid, Ciudad Real, Cuenca, Guadalara, Toledo.

The cookery of Castilla La Nueva centres round Madrid itself.

B

To Madrid are imported all the best products of Spain, the fish from the Mediterranean, the sherry from Jerez, the wines of Rioja and Valdepeñas, the grapes from Málaga and Andalucía, the vegetables from Valencia and the oysters from Galicia. Here are to be found restaurants 'tipicos' of all regions of Spain and of other countries, and moreover some of the best cooking in Spain. There is the Restaurant Casa Vasca for Basque cookery, el Hogar Gallego for Galician cooking, the Restaurant Meson Segovia from Segovia—where one eats excellent roast sucking pig, the Restaurant Bilbao for the fish dishes of Bilbao, La Tasca for any amount of typical Spanish dishes, the Valencia for the rice of Valencia, and many more which specialize in national and international dishes. The food of the Palace Hotel, the Playa, the Ritz and the Casa Hilton is all excellent, but on the whole more international than Spanish. In Escorial the Restaurant Felipe II has an outstanding cuisine with many national dishes of historical interest.

Madrid stands in the middle of a high plateau of mountainous, arid land with great extremes of temperature. Below Madrid is an arid level stretch of country extending to the south-east borders of Castilla la Nueva. This is La Mancha, the home of the fabulous Don Quijote. The town of Ciudad Real is the capital of La Mancha as well as of the province of that name. In this poor land, however, are produced the grapes and the wines of Valdepeñas. Wheat is cultivated in part of La Mancha and this explains the existence of Don Quijote's windmills. Sheep are also bred there and the famous Manchego cheese comes from La Mancha. It is excellent when fresh but becomes hard and dry when old and is not usually liked by foreigners when in this condition.

Dishes to ask for

CASTILLA LA VIEJA

Provinces: Burgos, Avila, Logroño, Santander, Segovia, Soria.

Part of this area is very fertile, while as we get near Castilla la Nueva in the south the land becomes mountainous and arid.

There is plenty of meat in the north, especially lamb and pig, chickens, turkey, rabbit and game, for it has fertile grazing land. Milk is good and there is an abundance of eggs and good river fish (trout, etc.), and in Santander salmon as well as sea fish such as besugo (a pink bream), anchovies, sardines, etc.

Burgos itself has a very good cuisine, and so has Soria.

Segovia is famed for its roast pig, which is excellently cooked at Meson Segovia.

Dishes to ask for

Soups *Page*

    Sopa de ajo: Garlic Soup   56

    Sopa Burgalesa: Burgos Soup (made of Lambs' Tails and River Crab)

Fish

    Truchas: Trout   138

    Bacalao con ajo de arriero: Dried Hake with Garlic, Tomato, etc.   114

    Anchoas Rebozados: Anchovies Dipped in Batter and Fried

    Anchoas en Cazuela: Anchovies Cooked with Onions   102

Meat

    Chorizo: Garlic and Pork Sausages with Red Pepper   42

    Cordero Asado: Roast Lamb   189

Poultry

    La Gallina en Pebre: Chicken in a Sauce   211

    Pavo en adobo: Stewed Turkey   216

    Conejo o Perdiz en escabeche: Soused Rabbit or Partridge   223

Sweets and Biscuits

    Rosquillas: Biscuits in the form of Rings   299

    Mantecados de Soria: Biscuits of Soria

    Yemas: Desserts made of Eggs and Sugar   318

    Torrijas: Like 'Pain Perdu'   288

    Biscocho de San Lorenzo: St Lawrence's Cake   312

EXTREMADURA

Provinces: Badajoz, Caceres.

Some of the best recipes come from this part of Spain; many of them originating from the old monastery at Alcántara.

Pheasants and partridges are world famous. Of the meat, pork is a speciality and also the sausages made from this pork. Lamb and kid are also plentiful. Truffles are found in this region. The most popular river fish are:

albure	dace
lamprea	lamprey
trucha	trout
sábalo	shad

Melons grow in abundance, especially the green-skinned, red-fleshed water melon (sandia).

Dishes to ask for

	Page
Soup	
Gazpacho Extremeño: Cold Vegetable Soup	76
Meat and Game	
Faisan al Alcántara: Pheasants à la Alcantara	225
Caldereta Extremeña: Stew of Kid or Lamb	197
Chorizo Extremeño: Pork and Garlic Sausage	42
Fish	
Bacalao al Alcántara: Dried Hake à l'Alcantara	116
Lamprea: Lamprey	
Truchas: Trout	
Albure: Dace	
Sábalo: Shad	
Eggs	
Tortilla de Chorizo Extremeño: Pork Sausage Omelette	83
Vegetables	
Judias y Patatas al Extremeño: French Beans and Potatoes	

Fruit
  Sandia: Water Melon
Sweets
  Turron: Nougat made of Almonds and Honey   315
  Mazapan: Marzipan
  Cabello de Angel: literally 'Angel's Hair'. A jam made
    from a gourd called sidra.   314

LAS BALEARES

Provinces: Mallorca, Menorca, Ibiza.

These three volcanic islands off the east coast of Spain have few natural resources. Mallorca has the most fertile land, as there is water in the mountains. The Arabs terraced the land and cultivated it, laying down a wonderful irrigation system. Tomatoes and grapes grow well. Ibiza is the most arid of the three islands. There are plenty of good fish in Mallorca but few in Ibiza. Meat is scarce in Ibiza, there being beef only. Mayonnaise obtained its name from the town of Mahon in Menorca.*

Dishes to ask for

Soups	*Page*
Sopa a la Mallorquina: Vegetable Soup	60
Sopa de Pescado: Fish Soup	68

Fish
  Atún a la Mahonesa: Tunny and Mayonnaise
  Langosta al estilo de Ibiza: Lobster à la Ibiza   149
Vegetables
  Tumbet: a mixed Vegetable Dish   264
Eggs
  Tortilla de Sardinas Frescas: Sardine Omelette   85

  * See introduction.

HERBS AND FLAVOURINGS IN SPANISH COOKING

The most common are:

perejil	parsley
hierbabuena	mint
ajo	garlic
laurel	bayleaf
orégano	wild marjoram
tomillo	thyme
comino	cumin seeds
mejorana	marjoram
guindilla	chili
azafrán	saffron
matalahuga	aniseed
alcaravea	caraway seed
ajonjoli	sesame
canela	cinnamon
clavo de comer	cloves
nuez moscada	nutmeg
salvia	sage (used only in the north of Spain)
alcaparra	caper

PEPPER. The pepper commonly used for flavouring is pimentón, which is the same as that known in England as paprika. Cayenne pepper (pimienta de cayenna) is rarely used except in the north. The ordinary ground black pepper is commonly used. Both it and white pepper (which is a luxury) are called pimienta. Black peppercorns (granos de pimienta) are used in stews. For further notes on pepper, see the chapter on Vegetables (page 231).

When using herbs and pepper as flavourings they should be discreetly blended so as to add to the flavour of the dish but not to overpower it and destroy it. In some cases one particular flavour should predominate. The use of herbs and flavourings is an individual matter and can be varied according to taste.

GARLIC and OLIVE OIL. Garlic used discreetly adds flavour to a dish, and many a time I have had people in my house who declare that they cannot possibly eat garlic, and yet, without knowing it, have eaten it quite happily in my dishes and have admired them. In fact, one must get over certain insular prejudices if one is going to enjoy the cookery of other nations. If the quantity of garlic given in any of these Spanish recipes seems excessive, then the remedy is to use less.

The oil in Spain is usually thick and unrefined, especially when young, and has a very penetrating odour. The Spanish usually brown garlic in the oil first and may or may not remove it. I have never found it gives a bitter flavour unless it is allowed to go black (there are recipes in the south of Spain in which this is done on purpose, to obtain the stronger flavour). Some cooks skin the garlic, some do not. Quite often the oil is 'fried' with the garlic in it and a little bread, and is then strained and bottled and kept to be used when required. This removes the strong odour of the oil and clarifies it.

SOME TYPES OF SPANISH SAUSAGES

CHORIZO. There are two types of sausage, one of which can be eaten raw and the other which can only be used in stews. The ones used in stews contain lean beef, lean and fat pork, red peppers and wild marjoram. The ones which are eaten raw are made of lean and fat pork with red and white pepper and garlic.

SALCHICHON. This is a delicious pork sausage made from fillet of pork, a little fat bacon and white pepper.

SALCHICHAS. These are made with a mixture of fillet of veal and pork, with white pepper, nutmeg and rum. They should be eaten when fresh.

LONGANIZA. Made with lean pork, garlic, wild marjoram, white pepper and salt.

BUTIFARRA. Made from fat pork, seasoned with salt, pepper, cloves, nutmeg and white wine.

MORTADELA. Made from lean pork, salt, spices, saltpetre, brown sugar and aguardiente.

MORCILLA BLANCA. This is made from chicken, fat bacon, hard-boiled egg, parsley, salt and spices.

MORCILLA ASTURIANA. This is a form of black pudding or blood sausage. The blood is mixed with pork fat, chopped onion, salt, red pepper, white pepper and marjoram.

WINES AND LIQUEURS

VINOS Y LICORES

'Bebo cuando tengo gana, cuanda no la tenga, y cuando me lo dan, por no parecer melindroso o mal criado.'
'I drink when I want to, when I don't want to and when I am given drink, in order not to appear prudish or badly bred.'

Sancho Panza, *Don Quixote*

The taste for wine is very individual and I can only give general hints on Spanish wines.

Spain is one of the oldest wine-producing countries in Europe. Its vineyards are as extensive as those of France, but the alcoholic content of the wine is higher. Its wines are numerous and many of them are not known outside the country. The Vino Tinto Corriente (red 'vin ordinaire') in many parts of Spain is better than the white and in Valencia, La Mancha and Galicia, among other provinces, it is often excellent. All over the south of Spain a 'sherry type' wine in barrel is drunk by the locals for a few pesetas a glass—i.e. a 'fino'.

Sherry is a wine which is world famous. There are various types such as Fino, Amontillado, Oloroso and Brown, going from light dry sherry to the heavy brown. In Spain, however, if one asks in a bar for an Amontillado they do not know what one means. 'Seco' or 'dulce' are the usual terms. 'Seco' is the Fino and Amontillado, and 'Dulce' the Oloroso or Brown. Manzanilla is very light and dry and, although not strictly speaking a sherry, is of the same family and comes from San Lucar.

Whereas most strangers drink dry sherry as an aperitif, many

Spaniards prefer the 'dulce'. It is best to know a few well-known brands and stick to them.

Many other wines, red and white, are known abroad; for instance the Riojas Red from the Rioja country round the valley of the Ebro. The wines of Valdepeñas, especially the red, are excellent in the country, but often do not travel well.

Tarragona produces a sweet and heavy wine like port.

Málaga produces Vino de Málaga, a dark brown wine, sweet and heavy, and a sweet Moscatel.

Montilla and Moriles produce a sherry-type wine. The wines of Galicia, such as Ribero, are good. Wine also comes from Toro, Zamorra and Navarre. Asturia produces a good cider.

Champagne Brut of the Casa Domecq, when obtainable, is an excellent drink. Spanish brandy is made from the 'lees' of the sherry fortified with alcohol and if one has a good brand is a pleasant drink. Any of the sherries of the well-known firms of Domecq, Williams & Humbert, Gonzalez Byass, Merito, Palomina and Vergara, etc are always good and reliable.

Here are a few suggestions for Spanish wines and liqueurs:

SHERRY (Vino de Jerez)
La Gitana: light and not too dry
Tío Pepe: very dry and not so good to drink in Spain as in colder climates
Solera 1847: a brown sweet sherry
Dry Sack: medium dry
Cándido: light and not so dry as Tío Pepe
San Hilario: medium brown
La Ina: a good light sherry
Jandilla: not so fine but good.

RED WINES (Vino Tinto)

The wines from Bodegas Bilbainas and Valdepeñas and Alella are good. Paternina, popularly known amongst tourists, is heavy and earthy and not to my taste. Cune is also heavy but cheap. The best everyday wines apart from the 'vino corriente' are the Riojas of Bodegas Bilbainas or a good Valdepeñas. The viño Pomal, Burgundy type, is excellent but more expensive. Good reliable wines for an occasion are those of Marques de Murrieta or Marques de Riscal, especially certain vintage years, about which any maître d'hôtel will advise you. Marfil (Alella) wine is also good but heavy.

WHITE WINES (Vino Blanco)

Viña Solè and Monopole are excellent and so is Cepa Rhin (gran reserva), all on the dry side.

Cepa Chablis (Paternina), a cheaper wine, varies considerably, but can be very good.

CHAMPAGNE (Champan)

Most of the Champagnes are too sweet but the Domecq's Champagne Brut is excellent.

COGNAC (Coñac)

Don't expect the same taste as French Brandy. The Brandy of Spain is distinctive but good brands make an excellent drink. 'Insuperable' is one of the kings of the Spanish cognacs but is often difficult to obtain, as is also 'Carlos I'.

The best after these are: Domecq's 'Fundador Champagne', Gonzalez Byass' 'Soberano' or Terry's 'Centenario', which is much heavier. Coñac Osborne, obtainable in the Seville region, is also good.

MALAGA WINES, etc
Malaga, Moscatel and Tarragón are all sweet and sickly.

LIQUEURS (Licores)
Calisay is one of the best of the Spanish liqueurs. Triple Seco resembles Cointreau and is very good. Creme de Cacao made in Barcelona is also pleasant. Annis Dulce (del Mono is the best) is a pleasant drink on all occasions. Annis Seco resembles Aquavit and is drunk before meals. It is drunk in Andalusia for breakfast by the peasant. They say that it 'mata los gusanos' (kills the worms). It is fierce and fiery but is certainly excellent drunk with coffee on a cold morning. 'Sol y sombra' (sun and shadow), equal parts of cognac and anis, is a good drink if you can stomach something fierce and make for a good siesta.

GIN
Larios produce one of the best gins but most Spanish gins are too sweet for foreign taste.
Italian type Vermouth, Benedictine and Green and Yellow Chartreuse are manufactured in Barcelona and are very good.

My thanks are due to Saccone & Speed, Ltd., for notes on the wines of Spain—my apologies for my personal prejudices.

SPANISH CHEESES

QUESOS

'Uvas con queso saben a beso'
Grapes and cheese taste like a kiss.

Spanish cheeses are not so good or so varied as those of France, principally because the average Spaniard has not much interest in them. The cheeses that one can find anywhere are:

MANCHEGO: the sheep's cheese of La Mancha, very good when fresh and soft.

QUESO DE CABRA: a goat's milk cheese, again good when freshly made.

QUESO DE BOLA: a cheese resembling the round red Dutch cheese made from cow's milk, and again only good when fresh and when it is not dry.

Galicia has many good local cheeses unknown outside the area. Many of the northern provinces have good local goat and sheep's milk cheese, which again do not keep. Ibiza has a cheese made from a mixture of goat and sheep's milk and the same remarks apply to it.

RESTAURANTS WHICH HAVE SUPPLIED RECIPES FOR THIS BOOK

Burgos	Restaurante Piñedo, Espoton 1
El Escorial	Hotel San Lorenzo de El Escorial
Granada	Hotel Victoria, Puerta Real
Lerida	Hotel Palacio S.A., Pateria 11 & 12
Logroño	Restaurante Adela, Calvo Sotelo 2
Guadalajara	Hotel España
Madrid	Meson del Segoviano, Cava Baja 36
Madrid	Palace Hotel
Palma de Mallorca	Oriente S.A. Ca'n Tomeu Paseo Generalisimo Franco 106
Santander	Las Caracoles, Medio 15 y Marina 1
Segovia	Restaurante Meson de Segoviano
Valencia	Restaurante Lara, Paz 46

RESTAURANTS AND HOTELS WHICH
HAVE SUPPLIED MENUS

Barcelona   Palace Hotel
Burgos   Hotel y Parador del Condestable
Lugo   Restaurante Fornos, General Franco 10
Teruel   Hotel Turia, Paseo de Generalisimo 1

HORS-D'ŒUVRE

HORS-D'ŒUVRE

Comiendo, comiendo el apetito se va abriendo.
Appetite increases with constant eating.

Entremeses (hors-d'œuvre) can vary from the simple conventional two or three hors-d'œuvre which precede a meal to the extensive tapas which are a meal in themselves, and which one can get in any little restaurant in Andalusia. Actually tapas are thought to have spoiled the cooking in Andalusia because people make their midday meal of them. Tapas are small snacks which one has with one's glass of sherry or vermouth. One can have just one or two or, as I say, make a complete meal of them. Typical examples are:

Olives, small or large, green or black.

Olives, stuffed with anchovies or pimientos.

Shellfish such as prawns; the deep-sea prawns (langostinos); cigalas (which are called langoustine in France); almejas (cockles) which are served cooked in a sauce with oil, chopped onion and garlic and parsley.

Tinned sardines and anchovies or fresh sardines and anchovies. These can either be fried or dipped in a batter or the sardines can be stuffed.

Tinned tunny fish.

Small fried pieces of whiting, hake, etc, and small pieces of fish in oil or tomato sauce.

Small pieces of meat, liver or kidney which have been fried in oil with a little garlic or are served in tomato sauce.

Salads of onion, tomato and red pepper (the tinned red peppers); cold chopped potatoes in vinaigrette or mayonnaise.

Small squids or calamares which are chopped in rings and fried, after being dipped in batter.

Small squares of goat's milk cheese or manchego (sheep's milk cheese).

Radishes.

Hard-boiled eggs in mayonnaise.

Potato crisps.

Slices of raw onion.

The delicious Serrano ham, which is Spanish smoked ham.

Different varieties of pâté.

Almonds or hazelnuts roasted in the oven.

Any variety of Spanish sausage, such as salchicha, salchichon, chorizo, etc (see page 42).

SOUPS

SOUPS

Sopas, lo mismo da muchas que pocas.
Soup—it doesn't matter if much or little.

The best Spanish soups are, I think, the fish soups which are found all round the coast. There is a good variety, and as the fish is fresh they are excellent in flavour. The next on the list are the cold soups; nothing is better on a hot day than a good iced Gazpacho or Sopa de Ajo Blanco. The Potajes, which are mostly the vegetable soups, are very satisfying and almost a meal in themselves.

Stock pots are noticeably absent in most of Spain, especially in the south. The Spanish Cocido usually supplies the meat soups; as will be seen later, the liquid from this stew is used as soup and the meat and vegetables are served separately.

Garlic soups are also numerous in different forms all over Spain. They are extremely nourishing as they must contain at least one egg per person.

CONSOMME DE GALLINA

CHICKEN CONSOMME

1 *small chicken, 2–3 lb, disjointed*
2 *lb breast of veal cut in pieces*
½ *teaspoon salt*
2 *sticks celery*
2 *leeks*
½ *teaspoon saffron*

2 *small turnips*
2 *carrots*
6 *egg yolks, well beaten*
6 *pints water*
6 *slices fried bread cut into small squares*

The legs, carcass and giblets of the chicken, together with the veal, celery, leeks, saffron, turnips and carrots are simmered for about 3 hours and seasoned with salt and pepper. The stock is then strained and clarified.

The egg yolks are beaten and mixed with a teacupful of the hot stock. They are then put in a buttered mould and cooked in a bain-marie. When set, the mould is taken out and left to cool and when cold the mould of eggs is cut into small pieces.

The wings and breast of the chicken are fried in oil and then skinned and boned.

The pieces of the egg mould, chicken and fried bread are then added to the clarified stock, reheated and served very hot.

For 8 people.

SOPA DE AJO MADRILEÑO

GARLIC SOUP OF MADRID

2 *tablespoons oil*	6 *thin slices bread cut into fingers*
6 *cloves garlic*	6 *eggs*
3 *pints water*	2 *or* 3 *tomatoes*
salt	½ *bayleaf*
½ *teaspoon paprika*	

The oil is heated in the pan and the cloves of garlic browned in it. The tomatoes and bayleaf are fried in the same oil, the boiling water is added and the soup seasoned and allowed to simmer for 15 minutes.

The slices of bread are placed in a large casserole and 6 eggs broken over them. The strained soup from the pan is then poured over them. The soup should then be placed in the oven until a brown crust forms on top, when it is ready to serve.

CONSOMME MADRILEÑO (MADRID)

This, I think, must be the refined version of Sopa de Ajo, onions being substituted for the garlic.

3 *pints good stock*	3 *beaten eggs*
3 *finely chopped onions*	3 *tablespoons oil*
1 *breakfastcup fresh breadcrumbs*	*seasoning*

The crumbs and chopped onion are fried in the oil and the eggs and seasoning added. This is well mixed together and allowed to cook until fairly solid and then allowed to cool. It is then formed into small balls which are fried in oil. These small balls are placed in the tureen, the consommé poured over them and the soup served immediately.

SOPA GRANADINA

GRANADA SOUP

3 *tomatoes*	3 *peppercorns*
2 *green peppers*	3 *cloves garlic, roasted in the oven*
3 *onions*	3 *slices bread cut in small squares*
oil for frying	*salt*
1 *sprig saffron*	

The onions, peppers and tomatoes are fried together in the oil. The saffron, peppercorns and roasted garlic are pounded together in a mortar and added to the fried vegetables. 3 pints of boiling water are then stirred in, and the soup simmered for about ten minutes, seasoned with salt, and served with squares of bread in it.

PURE DE GARBANZOS

PUREE OF CHICK-PEAS

1 *lb chick-peas, soaked overnight*   1 *sprig parsley*
2 *pints water*   1 *sprig thyme*
1 *onion*   6 *eggs*
1 *leek*   2 *oz butter*
1 *bayleaf*

These are all cooked together until the chick-peas are soft. The herbs, onion and leek are removed and the chick-peas and stock all passed through a fine sieve. The purée is reheated and then put on the side of the fire.

The eggs and the butter are gradually stirred into the purée which is carefully reheated, stirring well, and served.

This soup makes a very thick purée. The eggs and butter thin it down as they are beaten in at the side of the fire and are scarcely cooked. If the soup is too thick it can be thinned down to the required consistency by mixing in a little hot water.

For 6 people.

SOPA DE ALBONDIGAS A LA CATALANA (TARRAGONA)

CATALAN MEAT BALL SOUP

Some small meat balls (albóndigas) about the size of a marble are made. For these you require:

1 *cup minced lean meat*   1 *well-beaten egg*
½ *cup bread crumbs*   *salt and pepper*

These are well mixed together and shaped into little balls,
floured and fried.

FOR THE SOUP:

6 *slices of bread toasted in the oven*   4 *tablespoons tomato sauce*
1 *sprig parsley*   3 *pints stock*

The bread is placed in a large saucepan and the stock is poured
over it and heated. The tomato sauce is then stirred in and the
sprig of parsley added, together with the albóndigas and
seasoning. It is then cooked for half an hour on a moderate fire,
the sprig of parsley is removed and the soup is served.

For 6 people.

SOPA LEONESA (LEON)

SOUP LEONESA

¼ *lb beef dripping*   1 *stick cinnamon*
¼ *lb wheatmeal (semolina)*   *grated rind of half a lemon*
2 *pints milk*   3 *egg yolks*
1 *dessertspoon sugar*   3 *small slices bread fried in butter*

The beef dripping is melted and the wheatmeal stirred in and
allowed to cook slightly, stirring well. The hot milk, sugar and
cinnamon are then added with the grated lemon peel. This is

slowly cooked over a low fire for about 20 minutes, stirring from time to time and the cinnamon stick is then removed.

The saucepan is placed on the side of the fire, and the yolks, which have been previously beaten with a little warm milk, are added. They are well mixed and then the soup is poured over the pieces of fried bread, one in each soup plate.

Wheatmeal is like the very fine Italian semolina which is used for gnocchi and this can be found in England.

SOPA A LA MALLORQUINA

SOUP OF MALLORCA

3 *onions, sliced*
3 *red peppers, chopped*
1 *green cabbage, chopped*
2 *cloves garlic, chopped*
3 *peeled and seeded tomatoes, chopped*

1 *tablespoon chopped parsley*
salt
12 *thin slices bread*
oil for frying
2 *pints water*

Cover the bottom of the saucepan with oil and when hot add the onions, peppers, the green cabbage and garlic and allow it to cook gently. When the onion begins to soften add the tomatoes and parsley. Cover the pan and allow it to cook gently for about 15 minutes. Now add 2 pints of boiling water and bring to the boil again and simmer until the cabbage is soft.

Cover the bottom of a casserole, in which the soup will be served, with thin slices of bread. Then take out some of the vegetables and cover the bread with them. Then add another layer of bread and another of vegetables until all the vegetables have been taken out of the stock. The stock is now poured over this and allowed to simmer slowly. The whole of the stock should be absorbed, making a very solid purée.

For 6 people.

SOPA DE ALMENDRAS (GRANADA)

ALMOND SOUP

24 *almonds*	3 *peppercorns*
2 *pints water*	1 *teaspoon chopped parsley*
2 *tablespoons oil*	1 *teaspoon saffron*
3 *cloves garlic*	1 *red pepper*
2 *slices bread*	*salt*

The almonds are peeled and fried in hot oil and then removed and drained. The chopped garlic, bread, red pepper, parsley, peppercorns and saffron are all fried together in the same oil and then pounded in a mortar with the almonds. This mixture is then placed in a saucepan and the boiling water is gradually stirred in, seasoned with salt, and served.

CALDO DE PIMENTON (ALMERIA)

PEPPER SOUP

2¼ lb potatoes cut in thick slices
1 tomato
1 lb pollack or 'rape' (see p. 127) skinned and boned and cut in pieces
2 or 3 cumin seeds
2 cloves garlic

1 teaspoon saffron
1 dessertspoon paprika
3 green peppers grilled and skinned and cut in strips
6 pints water
salt
1 tablespoon oil

The potatoes are put in a deep saucepan in the water, seasoned with salt, together with the whole tomato. When the water is hot the fish is added and the tomato removed. The fish and potatoes are allowed to simmer.

Meanwhile the tomato is peeled and seeded and is ground down in a mortar with the cumin seeds, the garlic and the saffron and then a few pieces of potato are added and the paprika. The oil is gradually beaten into the mixture and then some of the stock from the pan is added, beating well all the time.

The whole of the sauce is then gradually added to the potatoes and the fish in the saucepan and stirred well until the potatoes are cooked. The green peppers are added just before the dish is finished.

SOPA DE ARAGON

SOUP OF ARAGON

½ lb calves' liver
¼ lb grated cheese
1 dessertspoon chopped parsley
½ teaspoon pepper

6 slices buttered toast about the
    size of half a postcard
3 pints of good stock
salt to taste

The calves' liver is simmered in a little water until cooked. It is then taken out, drained, and when cool it is minced finely and mixed with the grated cheese. The stock is gradually mixed into it and then the water in which the liver cooked. It is then seasoned and the parsley is added. This is gently brought to the boil, and when boiling the toasted buttered bread is placed on top of the soup. The pan in which the soup is cooking is then placed in the oven and left uncovered until a brown crust forms on the top.

In Spain a hard milk cheese is used. Parmesan is probably the best substitute in England. The Spaniards use equal parts of cheese and liver but in practice I found it is better to use ½ lb liver and ¼ lb cheese.

SOPA DE AJO (CADIZ)

GARLIC SOUP

5 cloves garlic
½ teaspoon salt
2 green peppers
1 teaspoon red pepper (paprika)

3 tomatoes, skinned and seeded
2 tablespoons oil
2 slices brown bread, without crust
1 pint water

Boil the tomatoes in the pint of water. The garlic, salt, green peppers (stalks and seeds removed), red pepper, tomatoes and oil are then pounded together and put into a saucepan. The bread and the boiling water in which the tomatoes were cooked are added alternately, mixing all the time until the bread is absorbed in the water and a thick purée results. This can easily be made in an electric mixer and reheated afterwards.

SOPA DE AJO CON MAYONESA (MALAGA)

GARLIC SOUP WITH MAYONNAISE

6 *cloves garlic, chopped and fried in oil*
16 *large cups boiling water*

6 *slices bread*
a mayonnaise made with 2 eggs

The chopped garlic is fried in the oil and then the boiling water is added, together with salt to season. The mayonnaise is added drop by drop, stirring all the time until all is well mixed in. Six slices of bread are cut into small squares, fried in oil, and added to the soup, which is then served.

SOPA DE AJO A LA ASMESNAL (SALAMANCA)

GARLIC SOUP À LA ASMESNAL

5 *cloves garlic*	6 *poached eggs*
oil for frying	3 *pints boiling water*
6 *small slices bread*	*some small pieces of cooked*
salt and pepper	*chicken*
1 *teaspoon chopped parsley*	1 *oz chorizo in small pieces*

The garlic is browned in the oil and removed. The bread is fried in the oil in a saucepan and then the boiling water is added, together with the parsley and seasoning.

The garlic is crushed in the mortar and replaced in the soup and stirred well. The pieces of cooked chicken and chorizo are added. One egg is placed in each soup plate and the soup poured over it.

For 6 people.

SOPA CASTELLANA SIGLO XIV (SEGOVIA)

CASTILIAN SOUP, FOURTEENTH CENTURY

$\frac{1}{4}$ *pint oil*	1 *coffeespoon red pepper (paprika)*
$\frac{1}{4}$ *lb ham, chopped*	*salt*
$\frac{1}{2}$ *lb bread*	2 *pints good stock*
2 *chopped cloves garlic*	6 *eggs*

The oil is heated in a saucepan and in this the chopped garlic

c

is browned and then the chopped ham is added and stirred well. The bread is cut in small slices and added to the pan; when browned, the red pepper is added, then the hot stock is stirred in, and cooked for 5 minutes. Turn out into a casserole. The eggs are now stirred in, the soup seasoned with salt and then placed in the oven for ten minutes.

For 6 people. From Restaurante Meson Cándido.

SOPA DE COLES A LA ASTURIANA (ASTURIAS)

CABBAGE SOUP A LA ASTURIANA

3 *lb of young cabbage*
½ *lb potatoes cut in small cubes*
2 *onions, finely chopped*
2 *cloves garlic, chopped*
3 *oz chorizo (garlic sausage) finely sliced*

2 *oz grated cheese*
4 *thin slices bread, halved and without the crust*
oil for cooking
salt and pepper
3 *pints water*

The garlic is browned in the oil in a frying pan and then removed. The onion is then slowly cooked in the oil and, when it begins to soften, the chorizo is added and the onion is allowed to brown slightly. The young cabbages are scalded in boiling water and then drained and the stalks removed. The leaves are cut into fine strips and with the potatoes are added to the frying pan and allowed to fry gently. The contents of the pan are then placed in a saucepan. Some boiling water is added to the frying pan and the pan is scraped well and this is added to the saucepan with the rest of the boiling water. The soup is seasoned and allowed to simmer gently for half an hour.

The bread is placed in a casserole and when the cabbage is soft the soup is poured over the bread, the grated cheese added and the casserole heated in a hot oven for ten minutes.

For 4–6 people.

CALDERADA

FISH SOUP OF GALICIA

$\frac{1}{2}$ *lb hake or ling*
$\frac{1}{2}$ *lb rape (see page* 127)
$\frac{1}{2}$ *lb pollack*
$\frac{1}{2}$ *lb gallina de mar (see page* 112)
4 *onions, finely chopped*
4 *cloves garlic, finely chopped*
1 *dessertspoon flour*

1 *dessertspoon parsley, chopped*
1 *dessertspoon vinegar*
1 *bayleaf*
1 *wineglass of oil*
salt and pepper
6 *slices bread, toasted in the oven*

This is a variety of Bouillabaisse. The fish is cleaned and cut in pieces of equal size. The oil, vinegar, flour, onions, garlic, parsley and bayleaf are placed in a casserole and the fish is added. The casserole is covered and then left for 2 hours. After this 4 pints of cold water are added and the seasoning, and it is cooked over a hot fire for 15–20 minutes. The liquid is strained off, reheated and poured over the slices of toast in a soup tureen. The fish is served separately.

SOPA DE PAN CON GAMBAS
(ANDALUCIA)

BREAD SOUP WITH PRAWNS

2¼ *lb prawns*
3 *tomatoes, skinned and seeded*
1 *green pepper*
1 *onion*
2 *cloves garlic*

thin slices of bread cut in 1 *inch*
   squares
saffron, pepper, salt
oil for frying

All the vegetables are finely chopped and then fried together in the oil. The prawns are cooked in about 3½ pints of water and then shelled. The water in which they were cooked is boiled and then gradually mixed with the fried vegetables. The prawns are added, the soup seasoned and cooked a few minutes. The bread is added at the last minute.

For 6 persons.

SOPA DE PESCADO

FISH SOUP

1 *lb fish*
4 *pints water*
2 *tomatoes*
4 *cloves garlic*
1 *large onion*

1 *red pepper*
1 *tablespoon chopped parsley*
2 *teacups fine breadcrumbs*
1 *dozen chopped almonds*
1 *dozen chopped hazel nuts*

The fish used can be a mixture of bream, whiting, hake etc, or it can be just one variety of fish.

The fish is skinned, the head and tail removed. It is then chopped into pieces, floured and fried in oil. The fish is then drained.

In the same oil the sliced tomatoes, onion, red pepper (stalk and seeds removed) and finely chopped garlic and parsley are fried. These are also drained.

The fried ingredients are all added to boiling water to which has been added 2 teacups of fine breadcrumbs and about a dozen each of finely chopped almonds and hazel nuts which have been previously browned in the oven. The soup is then allowed to simmer and when reduced by about a third is ready to serve. A refinement is to take out the large pieces of fish and to pass everything else through a fine sieve, then replace the fish in the soup, reheat and add salt and pepper as desired.

For 4 persons.

SOPA DE PESCADO CON MAYONESA (ANDALUCIA)

FISH SOUP WITH MAYONNAISE

For 1 lb white fish you need a mayonnaise made with 2 eggs.

The fish is boiled in $1\frac{3}{4}$ pints of salted water and then removed. The stock is then beaten gradually into the mayonnaise. The fish is added and reheated slightly.

SOPA DE OSTRAS (PONTEVEDRA)

OYSTER SOUP

4 *dozen small oysters*   *fried bread*
2 *pints fish stock*

The oysters are shelled and pounded in a mortar. They are then simmered in the stock for half an hour. The soup is then passed through a sieve and poured over about 12 small squares of fried bread in the tureen.

For 4 people.

SOPA DE CUARTO DE HORA (CADIZ)

QUARTER-OF-AN-HOUR SOUP

24 *'ostiones' (oysters can be used)*   1 *slice chopped ham*
1 *steak of hake (about ¼ lb)*   1 *chopped hard-boiled egg*
4 *oz prawns*   1 *tablespoon rice*
oil for frying   1 *teaspoon chopped parsley*
1 *small finely chopped onion*   *salt, pepper and red pepper*
1 *teacup picked peas*   *fried bread*
2 *tomatoes, skinned and seeded*

The oysters are cleaned, cooked in their shells until they open and then shelled. The water in which they have been cooked is kept.

The oil is heated in a saucepan and the onion and chopped ham are slowly fried in it, and then the chopped tomatoes. The red pepper is added together with the boiling water of the 'ostiones' (made up with boiling water to two pints). The hake —cut into small pieces—is added with the picked prawns, the shelled peas and the rice. The soup is salted and peppered and simmered for about twenty minutes. Then the oysters are added together with the finely chopped hard-boiled egg and the parsley. Squares of fried bread are served in the soup.

SOPA DE CUARTO DE HORA (MADRID)

QUARTER-OF-AN-HOUR SOUP

In order to show the variation in recipes of the same name in different parts of Spain, I am including this second recipe.

1 *large onion, chopped*	$\frac{1}{2}$ *lb hake, cut in small pieces*
2 *tomatoes, skinned, seeded and chopped*	$\frac{1}{2}$ *lb peas, already boiled*
	$\frac{1}{2}$ *lb mussels*
2 *cloves garlic, chopped fine*	2 *hard-boiled eggs, sliced*
1 *oz bacon, chopped fine*	8 *small squares of bread, toasted*
4 *deep-sea prawns, peeled and chopped*	*in the oven (about 2 inches square)*

The deep-sea prawns, hake and mussels are boiled together in about 2 pints of water with a little salt.

Meanwhile, the onion, garlic, tomatoes and bacon are slowly fried together in a little oil for 5 minutes. A little hot water from the fish is mixed in and then all is added to the saucepan. The sliced eggs are added, with the peas and toast, and it is cooked for a further 10 minutes on a low fire.

For 4 people. From the Palace Hotel.

SOPA DE RAPE (ANDALUCIA)

'RAPE' SOUP

'Rape' is a delicious Mediterranean fish with a firm white flesh
(see page 127).

1 *lb 'rape'*	10 *monkey nuts*
4 *tomatoes*	3 *cloves garlic*
2 *medium-sized onions*	*oil for frying*
1 *breakfastcup breadcrumbs*	1 *sprig parsley*
1 *bayleaf*	1 *teaspoon saffron*
the liver of the fish	*salt and pepper*
10 *hazelnuts*	

The fish is cleaned, cut in thick slices, and poached in water
with a small piece of lemon peel in it. The onions are chopped
and the tomatoes skinned, seeded and chopped. The onion is
gently fried in the oil and then the tomatoes with the nuts,
parsley, chopped garlic, saffron, the chopped fish liver and
breadcrumbs are all added and fried together. They are then
placed in a mortar (or in an electric blender) and pounded
together to a fine paste.

When the fish is practically cooked, the water is drained off,
made up to 3½ pints, and when boiling is gradually stirred into
the paste in a saucepan and allowed to simmer for half an hour.
The fish is then added and cooked for about five minutes
before the soup is served. A refinement is to remove the bones
and skin before placing the fish in the soup.

For 6 persons.

POTAJE DE GARBANZOS Y ACELGA

POTTAGE OF CHICK-PEAS AND SILVER BEET

(see page 235)

½ *lb chick-peas*	1 *bundle of silver beet or spinach*
1 *onion*	(1½ *lb of silver beet, or 2 lb*
1 *tomato*	*spinach*)
1 *bayleaf*	1 *tablespoon red pepper*
8 *cloves garlic*	*oil*
1 *sprig parsley*	2 *tablespoons wine or wine vinegar*

The chick-peas should be soaked overnight in water with a little salt in it. In the morning the peas will have swollen considerably and they should then be washed well and drained.

The chick-peas should then be put into two quarts of salted tepid water with the bayleaf, tomato, onion, 6 cloves of garlic, the parsley and the red pepper. Allow this to simmer, from time to time adding boiling water or stock to keep it at the same level.

After simmering for an hour add the washed leaves of the silver beet and simmer for another 20 minutes and then take out your onion and tomato and pass them through a sieve with the two uncooked cloves of garlic. Mix them with about 20 cooked chick-peas ground up in a mortar with 1 tablespoon oil. Dilute with a little of the soup, mixing well, and then pour back into the soup and simmer for about another 10 minutes.

Before serving add 2 tablespoons cooking wine or wine vinegar.

Enough for 6 persons.

POTAJE DE GARBANZOS

POTTAGE OF CHICK-PEA

½ lb chick-peas
3 tomatoes, skinned and
  seeded
1 large onion
2 tablespoons parsley
2 cloves garlic
1 bayleaf

1 dessertspoon red pepper
  (paprika)
1 teaspoon mixed spice
1 tablespoon curry powder
2 slices bread
salt and pepper
oil

Soak the chick-peas overnight in water with a little salt. Put them into a pan with 2 quarts of tepid water, bring to the boil and season.

Finely chop the onion, tomatoes, parsley and garlic. Cook the onion and garlic in a little oil without browning, then add the tomatoes, parsley, salt and pepper, the red pepper and crushed bayleaf and simmer gently. When this is a soft mass stir in a teaspoon of mixed spice and a tablespoon of curry powder and leave to cook gently for about another ten minutes.

Keep handy some boiling water to add to the chick-peas to keep at the two-quart level. Add some of the boiling water in which the chick-peas are cooking to the onion and tomato mixture and stir. Then stir all together and leave to cook for about another half an hour with the chick-peas.

Just before serving fry two slices of bread in oil and mince them. Add these to the soup. The yolk of a hard-boiled egg can be mixed with these crumbs if liked. If a thicker pottage is required, it can be left to reduce.

For 6 persons.

POTAJE DE HABAS SECAS (CORDOBA)

SOUP OF DRIED BEANS

¼ *lb fat bacon*
½ *lb pig's chap*
½ *teaspoon salt*
2 *cloves garlic*

1 *teaspoon curry powder*
1 *lb dried broad beans*
2 *quarts water*

Everything is placed in cold water and slowly cooked until the beans are tender.

POTAJE MADRILEÑO

POTTAGE OF MADRID

This is a soup which can be served on a fast day.

1 *lb chick-peas, soaked overnight*
1 *bundle spinach (about 2 lb)*
3 *pints water*
½ *teaspoon saffron*

1 *chili*
½ *lb bacalao (see page 114) soaked overnight and cut in small pieces*

The chick-peas are placed in the water and cooked until nearly tender, together with the bacalao and seasoning.

The spinach is cooked in boiling water which is then thrown away; the spinach is drained, chopped roughly and added to the soup.

The saffron and chili are ground down in a mortar and then mixed into the pottage.

GAZPACHO ANDALUZ

4 *tomatoes*
1 *small cucumber or half a large*
   one
3 *cloves garlic*
1 *teacup fine dry bread-*
   crumbs
1 *sweet red pepper*

3 *tablespoons oil*
$\frac{1}{2}$ *teacup wine vinegar or* 1 *dessert-*
   spoon vinegar
1 *onion*
$\frac{1}{2}$ *lb ice*
salt and pepper

The tomatoes, cucumber, red pepper and onion are minced. The garlic is pounded in a mortar and the salt, pepper and breadcrumbs are added. The oil is then added drop by drop until a thick paste is formed. The vinegar is slowly stirred in and this paste is placed in the soup tureen and the cucumber, etc, is mixed in. If a thinner soup is required a little water can be added.

It can all be mixed in an electric mixer and comes out like a purée, or if preferred, only the garlic, breadcrumbs, salt, pepper, oil and vinegar and a little water are placed in the mixer and then the chopped or minced vegetables are added.

For any method the ice is added and the soup left in a cold place. Finely chopped parsley can be added if desired.

Enough for 4–6 people.

GAZPACHO EXTREMEÑO

This Gazpacho differs from the Gazpacho Andaluz, as tomatoes, onions and green peppers are chopped finely and served apart.

Use the same quantities as for Gazpacho Andaluz but all the ingredients are pounded in a mortar or mixed in the electric mixer until a fine purée is obtained. Chopped cucumber, tomatoes, green pepper and cold squares of fried bread and chopped onion are served in separate little dishes on the table and can be added to the Gazpacho as required.

Enough for 4–6 people.

SOPA DE AJO BLANCO CON UVAS (MALAGA)

WHITE GARLIC SOUP WITH GRAPES

2 *tablespoons ground almonds or*   2 *tablespoons oil*
   30 *fresh almonds*   1 *tablespoon vinegar*
5 *cloves garlic*   1 *lb grapes, skinned and seeded*
½ *cup brown breadcrumbs*   1 *pint water*
salt   6 *ice cubes*

The original soup is made with fresh almonds, i.e. not green almonds but simply ripe ones recently removed from their shells and not kept for months. They are skinned, dried slightly in the oven and ground down in a mortar. Powdered almonds can be used but something of the flavour is lost.

The almonds and breadcrumbs are pounded in a mortar with the garlic and salt. The oil is added gradually, mixing well, then the vinegar. This mixture is put in the soup tureen and the water mixed with it, then the grapes are added and the ice, and it is left for about half an hour in a cool place.

For 6 persons.

SOPA DE AJO BLANCO

MELON SOUP

½ *teacup stale breadcrumbs*   1 *medium-sized yellow melon*
2 *tablespoons ground almonds*   1 *dessertspoon vinegar*
3 *cloves garlic*   ½ *lb ice*
2 *tablespoons oil*   *salt and pepper*

The bread is grated and the garlic is crushed with salt and
pepper. Then the almonds and breadcrumbs are pounded
together with the oil and garlic in a mortar, and the vinegar is
added.

The melon is skinned and chopped in slices about the size
of a finger. The mixture is poured over the ice in a soup tureen
and left to cool there together with the chopped slices of melon.

SALMOREJO (CORDOBA)

This is a form of gazpacho used by the poor people.

It is made simply with garlic, salt, breadcrumbs, oil and
vinegar all pounded together as for gazpacho, with a little
water added. On special occasions, instead of the bread, hard-
boiled eggs are used and a little tomato.

There is a more sophisticated version called Carnerete. The
bread and eggs are fried and then pounded in a mortar with
the garlic, etc, and the soup is made as above.

EGG DISHES

EGG DISHES

El huevo fresco y el pan moreno.
Eggs must be fresh and bread must be brown.

OMELETTES AND EGG DISHES

The Spanish Tortilla or Omelette is quite unlike its French cousin. It is a solid satisfying concoction which can be eaten hot or cold. It can be taken on picnics between slices of bread or in a roll.

Egg dishes are extremely varied and are mixed with vegetables, etc, rather like some of the dishes in the south of France. The following are some typical examples.

TORTILLA ESPAÑOLA

SPANISH OMELETTE

3 *eggs, well beaten*   *oil*
2 *medium-sized potatoes*   *salt and pepper*
1 *small onion*

The potatoes are chopped finely, like match-sticks, and the onion is also chopped. Both are fried slowly in the oil, without browning, until tender. The beaten eggs are then added and fried. The omelette is turned over and cooked on the other side (the easiest way is to put a plate on top and turn the frying pan upside down, the omelette is then slipped back in the pan on the other side).

Instead of potatoes and onion, asparagus, artichokes, ham or peas can be used as a filling.

TORTILLA ALCARREÑA (MADRID)

OMELETTE ALCARREÑA

3 *asparagus tips*   1 *slice smoked Spanish ham*
1 *large potato*   3 *eggs*
1 *slice chorizo*

All the ingredients are coarsely chopped and heated gently in a little butter in a frying pan until partially cooked. The beaten eggs are then poured over them, and the omelette cooked in the same way as a Spanish Omelette.

From Hotel España, Guadalara.

TORTILLA DE SESOS

BRAIN OMELETTE

Calves' brains are used for this. One needs only a few small pieces, according to taste.

They are first boiled with a little vinegar, parsley and onion and seasoning. They are then drained and mixed with the well-beaten eggs and cooked as for other tortillas.

TORTILLA DE CHORIZO EXTREMEÑO (EXTREMADURA)

OMELETTE OF CHORIZO EXTREMENO

6 *slices of chorizo (pork sausage)*	*3 eggs* *oil for frying*

The chorizo is fried a little in the oil then the beaten eggs are added and an omelette made as other tortillas.

For 2 persons.

TORTILLA MESON DE CANDIDO (SEGOVIA)

OMELETTE MESON DE CANDIDO

6 *sticks asparagus*	¼ *lb ham, chopped*
¼ *lb shelled peas*	12 *eggs*
2 *oz green peppers, chopped*	½ *pint oil for frying*
2 *oz French beans, sliced*	100 *grammes pickled fish*
¼ *lb chorizo, chopped*	*(escabeche)*

The oil is heated in a large pan and all ingredients except the eggs are cooked in it. When everything is hot and well amalgamated, the beaten and seasoned eggs are added. This omelette is made in the form of a French omelette and not a Spanish one, so should be made in two halves, as the quantities would be too much for the normal omelette pan.

For 6 people. From the Restaurant Meson de Cándido.

TORTILLA MURCIANA

MURCIAN OMELETTE

2 *sweet red peppers, skinned,*   3 *tomatoes, skinned, seeded and*
seeded and chopped   *chopped*
4 *eggs*   *oil for frying*

The eggs are well beaten. The oil is heated in the pan and the
tomatoes and red peppers cooked together in the oil until fairly
soft. Any excess of oil can be poured off before adding the eggs.
The eggs are poured in and it should be cooked on a lower fire
than a French omelette and should be solid.

See instructions on Spanish Omelette (page 81).

TORTILLA AL SACROMONTE

SACROMONTE OMELETTE

This is a famous Granada dish.

1 *calf's brain*   3 *medium-sized potatoes,*
oil for frying   *finely chopped*
2 *calf's or sheep's sweet-*   1 *cup shelled cooked peas*
breads   6 *eggs*
1 *egg for coating*   *salt and pepper*

The brain is cleaned, skinned and boiled, then drained and
allowed to cool. It is cut into small pieces about the size of a
walnut, egg-and-breadcrumbed and fried in oil. It is again

allowed to cool and is then chopped into smaller pieces the size of a pea.

The sweetbreads are washed, seasoned, chopped fine and left to drain. The potatoes are fried, then all the ingredients are mixed with the beaten eggs which are cooked in a large frying pan and emerge as a firm Spanish omelette.

TORTILLA DE SARDINAS (BALEARES)

SARDINE OMELETTE

½ *lb fresh sardines, cleaned and*   1 *clove garlic*
  with the heads, tails and bones   1 *dessertspoon chopped parsley*
  removed   1 *teaspoon paprika*
3 *eggs*   *juice of* 1 *lemon*

The yolks are well beaten with a little salt and parsley. The whites are also well beaten with salt. A deep frying pan is heated and the bottom covered with oil. In this oil the crushed garlic is fried. Half the yolks and half the whites are placed in the pan and the whole surface is covered with the sardines and then the remaining eggs, seasoned with pepper and lemon juice, are poured over the sardines. A little hot oil is sprinkled on top. This is then cooked fairly slowly until brown. It is then, if possible, turned into a second frying pan to brown on the other side.

HUEVOS A LA FLAMENCA (SEVILLA)
EGGS À LA FLAMENCA

6 *eggs*
3 *tomatoes, sliced*
2 *large red peppers*
3 *slices dried Spanish ham,*
   chopped in small pieces
6 *slices chorizo (pork sausage)*
½ *cup cooked peas*

½ *cup French beans (cooked)*
1 *large onion, sliced*
2 *cloves garlic, chopped*
salt and pepper
1 *teaspoon chopped parsley*
oil

The garlic and onion are fried in the oil and when they are a little tender the ham and tomatoes are added. When these are cooked, the peas, beans and chorizo are added. Add salt and pepper and divide into three parts. The mixture is put in three small oven plates. Two eggs are put on top of each plate and baked in the oven with a few slices of red peppers and the parsley sprinkled over them. If wished all can be cooked together in one large dish.

HUEVOS EMPANADAS

Poach 6 eggs and drain them. Dip them in flour, beaten egg and breadcrumbs and fry.

HUEVOS AL NIDO

EGGS IN NESTS

4 *eggs*
4 *slices bread, about ½ inch thick,*
  without crust

4 *tablespoons milk*
1 *oz butter*
salt and pepper

A hole is made in the centre of each slice of bread, without completely going through the thickness of the bread. A tablespoon of milk is gently poured in each hole and allowed to soak in. The bread is now thinly spread with butter and a little dab of butter put in each hole and the yolk of an egg placed on top and seasoned with salt and pepper. The whites of the eggs are well beaten and then a ring of white is placed round each egg. Each slice of bread with the egg on top of it is carefully placed in a frying pan of deep oil. The oil is spooned over the white so that it browns. When the white is brown, each slice is removed and carefully drained on a cloth.

This can be served as it is or with tomato sauce in a sauceboat.

For 4 people.

HUEVOS AL PLATO (ALAVA)

EGGS À LA PLATO

2 *sliced tomatoes*
1 *chopped clove garlic*
1 *chopped teaspoon parsley*
salt
2 *eggs*

3 *thin slices white morcilla, fried*
   (see page 42)
2 *tablespoons grated cheese*
oil for frying

The morcilla is fried in the oil and removed. The tomatoes, garlic and parsley are fried together and then placed in the bottom of a small greased earthenware or pyrex dish, which can be served at table. The eggs are broken over the mixture and the sausage is laid between the yolks. The cheese is sprinkled on the yolks before serving.

For 1 *person.*

CAZUELA DE ESPINACAS CON HUEVOS A LA GRANADINA

A DISH OF SPINACH AND EGGS À LA GRANADINA

The spinach must have large green and tender leaves. The best comes from the Carennes Albaycinenon of the Morisca at Granada.

1 *lb spinach*
20 *almonds, skinned*
2 *cloves garlic*
2 *slices bread, without the crust*
½ *teaspoon saffron*
1 *clove*
2 *peppercorns*
2 *cumin seeds*
1 *pint stock*
6 *eggs*
½ *lb ham*

The spinach is well washed and then cooked slowly for about 20 minutes. It is taken out, the water pressed out of it and left to drain.

The saffron, clove, peppercorns and cumin seeds are ground down in a mortar with a pestle and then about 1 tablespoon of water is added to make a thick paste and this is put in a bowl on one side.

The almonds, garlic and bread are fried in the oil and then also pounded down in the mortar and mixed with the paste.

The well-drained spinach is finely chopped and mixed with the other ingredients in a deep wide pan which can be placed in the oven. Hot stock, about 1 pint, is gradually mixed in to form a thick purée. The eggs are broken on top of the purée, and the ham—cut in julienne strips—is placed round them. The dish is then heated in a hot oven for about ten minutes until the eggs have set.

From the Hotel Victoria.

HUEVOS DE PRIMAVERA

SPRING EGGS

1 *small green cabbage*
1 *egg of butter*
3 *French leaf artichokes*
4 *rashers ham, chopped*
½ *lb French beans*
4 *red peppers, quartered*

1 *bundle asparagus*
1 *cup tomato sauce*
1 *breakfastcup picked peas*
2 *tablespoons grated cheese*
12 *eggs*

The vegetables are all par-boiled separately. They are then well drained; the cabbage, artichokes and French beans are chopped and the cooking is completed in a pan with the butter, ham and red peppers. The tomato sauce is finally mixed in.

When cooked this is placed in a flat open oven dish. 12 eggs are broken over it. They are seasoned and sprinkled with cheese and then cooked in the oven.

HUEVOS TORTOLA (VALENCIA)

'TURTLE DOVE' EGGS

4 *French leaf artichokes*
1 *hen's liver*
juice of half a lemon
1 *bunch spinach* (2 *lb approx*)
water to cover

salt
1 *egg of butter*
4 *eggs*
4 *tablespoons grated cheese*

The artichokes are cleaned and quartered and the spinach well washed and chopped. They are then placed in a saucepan together with the chopped hen's liver, salt and lemon juice and sufficient water to cover them. They are cooked on a slow fire and, when ready, the water is strained off and the butter mixed in.

The eggs are broken into a flat dish and then covered with the mixture. The cheese is grated on top and the dish is then allowed to brown in the oven.

HUEVOS ARRIBA ESPAÑA

1 egg
1 square bread—about 4 inches
   by 4 inches
1 oz grated gruyère cheese

butter
a little cayenne pepper
salt

The bread is toasted in the oven and then buttered. One yolk is placed in the centre of the bread. The white is stiffly beaten with the cheese. It is then piled on the toast, covering the yolk, and then sprinkled with cayenne and salt. It is baked in a moderately hot oven.

For 1 person.

HUEVOS BECHAMEL EMPANADAS

EGGS FRIED WITH BÉCHAMEL

4 eggs
white breadcrumbs
salt and pepper
1 pint milk

$\frac{1}{4}$ lb butter
$\frac{1}{4}$ lb flour
1 beaten egg

The eggs are poached and then trimmed, or they can be boiled so that the whites are hard and the yolks soft. They are then put on one side to cool. A béchamel is made with the butter, flour and milk. It is seasoned and then, when cool, each egg is covered with this. They are then dipped in beaten egg, rolled in breadcrumbs and fried in oil. Serve with a sprig of rosemary on each egg.

For 4 people.

HUEVOS CON MARISCOS

EGGS WITH SCALLOPS

Mariscos literally means shellfish, but in this case it is a small smooth-shelled scallop.

The scallop is put in a hot oven until the shell opens and then is removed from its shell.

Allow one scallop per person.

juice of ½ lemon	*a little oil for cooking*
2 eggs	*½ dozen deep-sea prawns,*
1 dessertspoon milk	*shelled*
salt and pepper	*1 tablespoon chopped parsley*

The scallop is covered with the lemon juice and left for 20 minutes. The eggs are beaten with the milk and seasoned. They are then placed in the saucepan with the chopped scallop and cooked over a slow fire. Serve surrounded with prawns and sprinkled with parsley.

An ordinary scallop can be used, although it is larger than the Spanish one, and ordinary prawns can replace the deep-sea ones.

FISH

Mentir y comer pescado quieren cuidado.
To lie and to eat fish needs care.

There is an abundance of fish round the coast of Spain, many varieties of which we do not know in England, and which make extremely good eating. Fish, for the most part, is fried only—the small fish whole and the larger fish in fillets. Or it may be cooked whole in oil on top of the stove or in the oven, covered with chopped onion, garlic, tomatoes, slices of lemon, etc. The dried cod (bacalao), if properly cooked, is extremely good. It is a pity that so many visitors to Spain only want fried sole or hake, when there are so many excellent fish dishes.

It is extremely difficult to give a clear description of the fish found in Spanish waters, some being completely unknown in England and having no translation for their names. An added difficulty is that the same fish varies in name in different regions in Spain, and even at times from village to village. I have endeavoured to give a fairly broad picture of the fish and their type of cookery. For those who are interested, here is a brief division of the fish into their different families:

SHELLFISH (*'marisco' is the general term*)
  Crustaceans
  Bogavante   Lobster.
  Langosta   Sea Crayfish.
  Cangrejo   Crab (small sea and river).
  Centolla   Spider Crab.
  Camarón   Shrimp.
  Gamba   Prawn.

| Langostina | Deep-sea Prawn. |
| Cigala | Dublin Bay Prawn. |

Mollusc (which may be bivalved or univalved)

Caracol	Sea Snail.
Caracol	Land Snail.
Almejas	Cockles.
Almejones	Scallops.
Mejillones	Mussels.
Marisco Liso or Morcillón	Smooth-shelled small Scallops.
Ostras	Oysters.
Ostion	A form of Oyster.

FAMILY MERLUCIDES

| Merluza | Hake or Ling. A favourite with foreigners. Rather strong flavour. |

FAMILY URANOSCOPIDES

| Rata del Mar | Common Star-gazer. Used in stews, etc (see page 129). |

San Pedro (Gallo in Andalusia)	John Dory. Excellent eating.
Pez de Espada (or Aguja Palá)	Sword Fish. Excellent eating.
Anguila	Eel.
Angula	Small river Eel.

FAMILY SCOMBRIDES

| Caballa (or Verdel) | Mackerel. Dark red flesh, not good eating. |

Estornino	Spanish Mackerel. Pinkish white flesh, good to eat.
Atun	Tunny fish. Pinkish flesh. Usually found tinned in Spain and good to eat in this form.
Atun Africano	African Tunny.
Albacora and Bacoreta	Other forms of Tunny.
Bonito	Bonito. Excellent eating.

FAMILY SCORPENIDAE

Rascasio	Rock Fish. This fish is mostly dark red and has an ugly big head and gills. Used in fish soups, etc.
Gallineta	Sand Piper. A rock fish which resembles Rascasio and is a greyish colour. Very good cooked in the oven.
Cabracho	No translation. An extremely ugly fish with a large head, dark red in colour with spots, very like Rascasio. A delicate flavour, good baked in the oven.

FAMILY GADIDAE

Brótola de Roca	Resembles Burbot.
Abadejo	Pollack. Good; can be cooked like Bass.
Faneca	Pout. Resembles Pollack but not very good to eat.
Molléra	Power Cod. Resembles Faneca, coarse flesh.
Brótola de Fango	Great Forked Beard. Fair eating.

D

Pescadilla	Whiting. Large, and better eating than the English Whiting.

FAMILY SCEINIDES

Corvina (or Corballo)	No translation. Coarse and not very good.

FAMILY TRIGLIDES

Rubio	Red Gurnard. A red fish with a large ugly head. Fairly good eating.
Garneo	Piper. Resembles Gurnard.
Carpón (or Gallina del Mar)	Red fish with a large head and enormous gills. Excellent eating.

FAMILY LOPHIDES

Rape	Angler Fish or Frog Fish. White flesh, resembles Skate in appearance and makes excellent eating.

FAMILY SQUATINIDES

Angelote	Monk Fish. Like Rape in appearance but not so good to eat.

FAMILY RACIDES

Raya	Skate. Several varieties are found.

FAMILY SPARIDES (*the Bream family*)

Boga	Bogie. Poor eating.
Saupa (or Salema)	No translation. Good eating.
Sargo	Grey Bream. Rather dull eating.
Dorada	Gilthead. Similar to Sargo, with black mark and gold stripe on head. Good to eat.
Raspallón	Grey Bream. Dull eating.

Oblada	Grey Bream. Dull eating.
Besugo	Small Pink Bream. Dull eating.
Pargo	Red Bream. Excellent eating.
Pagel (or Breca)	Pandora or Spanish Bream. Good to eat.
Chopa	Bream, dark grey with black marks. Good to eat.
Besugo de Laredo	Red Gilthead. Fair eating.

FAMILY CARANGIDES

Jurel (Trachurus Trachurus)	Mackerel? It is not of the Mackerel family but most resembles the English Mackerel in appearance.
Pez de Limón	Mediterranean Silver Fish. Very good.
Palometa	No translation. Fair eating.
Palometón	No translation. Fair eating.

FAMILY CLUPEIDES

Sardinas	Sardines. Good to eat.
Sabalo (or Alosa)	Shad. Good to eat.
Alacha	Large Sardine. Not so tasty as a Sardine.
Espadin	Sprat. Cured like Sardines.

FAMILY ENGRAULIDES

Boquerón (or Anchoa or Bocarte)	Anchovy. Excellent to eat fresh.

FAMILY SERRANIDES

Mero	Rock Bass. Excellent.

Lubina (or Robalo— Latin Morone Labrax)	Bass. Excellent.
Baila	Sea Trout. Not so tasty as Bass.
Serrano	No translation. Reddish orange fading to white below, with black dorsal stripe and several vertical stripes. Good to eat.
Vaquita (or Cabrilla)	No translation. Like Serrano, but is poor eating.
Doncella	Another form of Bass. Fair eating only.
Jabali (or Rayón)	Of the Bass family, not unlike Mero. Good eating.
Cherna	No translation. Grey with brownish markings, often mistaken for Mero.
Margota (or Jaroba or Bullon de Roca)	Wrasse. Excellent. Cook like Bass.

FAMILY MUGOLIDES

Mujol (or Albur or Mugle)	Mullet. Grey, with black horizontal bands. Fairly good—the roe is the best part.
Lisa	Grey Mullet. Excellent eating.
Salmonete	Red Mullet. Excellent when large, but is usually caught too small and is tasteless.

FAMILY PLEURONECTIDES

Rodaballo	Turbot. Rather coarse.

Gallo	Thinner and more oval than Turbot, with a pigmented skin. Good eating.
Platija	Plaice. Not found in the south of Spain. Both eyes on right flank instead of head. Not so good as Sole.

FAMILY CONGRIDES

Congrio and Zafio	Conger Eel. Very good eating, rather like Hake but better.

FAMILY BRAMIDES

Japuta	No translation. Found in the north of Spain: a black fish, 15–20 inches long, fished in the winter with nets.

FAMILY TRACHINIDES

Araña	Weaver. Rarely caught on account of its poisonous spines. Pretty rainbow colours, with blue predominating. Flesh firm and good to eat.

BOQUERONES

ANCHOVIES

These are floured and joined by their tails and fried in the form of a fan.

ANCHOAS EN CAZUELA (BASQUE)

CASSEROLE OF ANCHOVIES

The bottom of a wide and fairly deep saucepan is covered with oil and sprinkled with chopped onion. On this is placed a layer of fresh anchovies, then more chopped onion, then anchovies and so on, finishing with the anchovies. It is then sprinkled with oil and paprika and cooked slowly until the anchovies are soft. Sardines can be cooked in the same way.

ESCABECHE DE BOQUERONES

SOUSED ANCHOVIES

2¼ *lb fresh anchovies*
6 *cloves garlic*
2 *sprigs saffron*
1 *teaspoon cumin seeds*
1 *teaspoon ground ginger*
½ *pint wine vinegar*

½ *pint water*
salt
1 *lemon, sliced*
2 *bayleaves*
flour mixed with salt for
  coating

The anchovies are cleaned and washed and then floured. The tails of three or four are crossed and they are fried in oil and drained.

In the same oil the garlic is fried and then, together with the saffron, cumin and ginger, ground down in a mortar; the vinegar is gradually added, then the water and salt. The anchovies are placed in a deep pan and the spice and vinegar mixture poured over them. The slices of lemon and the bayleaves are laid on top. This is left for 24 hours before being eaten.

LUBINA

BASS

The fish is seasoned and put on a buttered oven dish. When half cooked it is sprinkled with lemon juice and finely chopped parsley. Just before serving it is sprinkled with finely chopped hard-boiled egg.

It can also be poached, skinned and boned and allowed to cool. It is then served with mayonnaise or a vinaigrette.

BESUGO

BREAM

These are the small bream with the pinkish head. They are bony and not very good. They are best fried whole and served with lemon; or filleted, egg-and-breadcrumbed and fried.

BESUGO A LA DONOSTIARRA (BASQUE)

SMALL RED BREAM À LA DONOSTIARRA

2¼ *lb red bream*　　　　　1 *dessertspoon lemon juice*
3 *tablespoons oil*　　　　　*salt*
2 *cloves garlic*

The bream are cleaned and salted and left in a cool place for an hour before serving. They are then placed on a grill, painted with oil, and turned repeatedly until the skin is nicely browned. Before serving they are sprinkled with hot oil mixed with lemon juice and grated garlic.

BESUGO A LA PASTELERA

RED BREAM À LA PASTELERA

2 *lb bream*
1 *lemon, sliced*
1 *dessertspoon chopped parsley*
salt and pepper
1 *teacup white breadcrumbs*

oil to cover the pan
2 *cloves garlic, chopped*
½ *teaspoon red pepper (paprika)*
1 *wineglass good dry sherry or*
  white wine

Clean the bream and incise the skin every 2 inches and put the slices of lemon in the slits.

Lay the bream in an earthenware dish, which is just covered with the oil. Sprinkle the crumbs, parsley, garlic and pepper over it and sprinkle with a little more oil. Bake in a moderate oven and when cooked add the sherry and serve in the same dish.

For 4 people.

BESUGO ASADO CON PIRIÑACA

RED BREAM BAKED IN 'PIRIÑACA'

Piriñaca is a mixture of tomatoes, onion, paprika, garlic, bay-leaf, parsley and cucumber chopped with oil and vinegar or lemon.

2¼ *lb bream*
1 *onion*
3 *cloves garlic*
1 *bayleaf*
1 *dessertspoon chopped parsley*
2 *tablespoons oil*

1 *sweet green pepper*
3 *tomatoes*
juice of half a lemon
½ *small cucumber*
salt

The cucumber and tomatoes are sliced. The onion, garlic, bay-leaf and pepper are chopped finely. The bream are placed whole on a greased fireproof dish. The slices of tomato and cucumber are placed on the fish. The rest of the ingredients are mixed with the salt, lemon juice and oil and sprinkled on the top. The fish is then baked in the oven.

PARGO

LARGE RED BREAM

The large deep-sea bream are much more tasty than the besugo. They are best cooked whole and can be poached; or baked in the oven lying on sliced potatoes and onions, covered with slices of lemon, tomato and red peppers and covered with buttered paper. They are served in the same dish.

PARGO ENCEBOLLADO (ANDALUCIA)

2¼ *lb deep-sea bream*   1 *tablespoon pounded walnuts*
4 *onions*   *oil*
4 *tomatoes*   3 *sweet green peppers*
5 *cloves garlic*   *salt and pepper*
1 *sprig parsley*

The tomatoes are skinned, seeded and quartered. The walnuts are pounded in a mortar and mixed with the finely chopped onion, garlic and parsley. The peppers are sliced.

The bottom of an oven dish is covered with oil. Half the chopped mixture is sprinkled over it and the fish is laid on top. It is then seasoned with salt and pepper, the rest of the chopped mixture is spread over it and finally the whole is covered with the sliced peppers and tomatoes, and sprinkled with oil.

The dish is covered and cooked slowly in the oven. When the fish is cooked the dish is uncovered and the sauce allowed to evaporate a little. Serve in the same dish.

ATUN O BONITO CON TOMATES (HUELVA)

TUNNY OR BONITO WITH TOMATOES

2¼ *lb fish*   1 *tumbler white wine*
oil for frying   ½ *cup breadcrumbs*
1 *teaspoon sugar*   1 *tablespoon chopped parsley*
3 *cloves garlic, finely chopped*   *salt and pepper*
1 *onion, finely chopped*   1 *teaspoon paprika*
3 *tomatoes, seeded and skinned*

The fish is cut in thick steaks, seasoned, and fried in a frying pan with as little oil as possible.

In another saucepan the onion and garlic are slowly cooked in oil and then the tomatoes are added, together with the white wine and parsley; the whole mixture is covered and simmered slowly for two hours.

When the fish is fried it is drained well and put in a casserole or oven dish. The breadcrumbs are then slowly fried in the oil in which the fish was cooked, and when nicely browned the paprika is added. This is then added to the tomato mixture and everything is stirred well. This thick sauce is now passed through a sieve, seasoned with salt, pepper, and the sugar and poured over the fish, which is cooked uncovered in the oven for about ten minutes and then served in the same dish.

For 4–6 persons.

MARMITA (BASQUE)

STEW OF BONITO

2¼ *lb bonito, cut into small pieces*   1 *lb sliced potatoes*
oil to cover the bottom of the pan   *salt and paprika*
2 *large onions, chopped*   3 *red peppers (tinned)*
3 *cloves garlic, chopped*   3 *slices bread cut in 2-inch*
4 *pints water, boiling*   *squares*

The onion and garlic are gently cooked in the oil in a deep saucepan. The pieces of fish are added and, when browned slightly, the boiling water and potatoes are added and simmered until the potatoes are cooked. The marmite is then seasoned with paprika and salt and the chopped red peppers are added. The squares of bread are added at the last minute.

BROTOLA DE ROCA

This is a grey fish with reddish fins, about 8–10 inches long, of the cod family. It resembles a burbot. It is best cooked whole in the oven in an oiled dish with slices of lemon, tomato, onion, grated garlic and parsley on the upper surface. Cover with greaseproof paper and bake. It can also be cut in thick slices, dipped in flour and fried, or it can be used in soups, rice dishes, etc.

CALDERETE ASTURIANA (ASTURIA)

A FISH STEW

3 lb fish (a mixture of bass, red mullet, bream)
12 deep-sea prawns
12 lapas (a kind of oyster)
2 tablespoons oil
3 finely chopped onions
1 teaspoon paprika
2 tablespoons parsley
6 peppercorns
½ tumbler medium sherry
½ teaspoon nutmeg
2 paprikas, ground down in a mortar
1 capsicum (chili pepper), chopped
2 quarts boiling water

The fish are cleaned and their heads and tails removed. The small fish are left entire and the large ones are cut in thick slices. The prawns are shelled and the 'lapas' cooked in water and shelled. The fish is placed in the saucepan with the oil and the chopped onion and allowed to sweat slowly for about 5 minutes. The boiling water is then added and the calderete is seasoned with the salt and pepper and is simmered for another 5 minutes. The rest of the ingredients are then added and the cooking continued for a further 15 minutes or until all the fish is cooked.

MOYA

'COD'

Moya is of the cod family. Its flesh is coarse and not very savoury. A whole fish can be cooked in the oven in the following way:

Butter a fireproof dish and cover the bottom of it with sliced potatoes and onions; half-cook in a moderate oven. Lay your fish on this. Put on it a few slices of lemon, tomatoes, chopped parsley and garlic, and sprinkle with sherry. Cover with buttered paper and bake.

Moya can also be cooked in the same way as any other type of cod.

CONGRIO O SAFIA

CONGER EEL

Stuffed. Remove the spine and bones and stuff with forcemeat as for sardines (see page 131) and then bake in a buttered dish in the oven, covered with buttered paper. 1 lb takes about half an hour.

Poached. The fish can be poached and served hot, or cold with mayonnaise.

Fried. The eel is cut in steaks like hake, egg-and-breadcrumbed and fried.

GALLO O SAN PEDRO

JOHN DORY

These fish with the large ugly head and the mark of St Peter's thumb on them make delicious eating.

They should be baked whole in the oven covered with slices of lemon, a little chopped garlic and onion, and sprinkled with white wine and oil.

ANGUILAS

EELS

Eels can be cleaned and skinned, cut in slices, seasoned, floured and fried.

SALPICON DE ANGUILAS LARA
(VALENCIA)

EEL IN SAUCE

6 *small eels cut in two or three*   *white and red pepper (paprika)*
   pieces   12 *almonds*
oil for frying   1 *dessertspoon chopped parsley*
salt   2 *cloves garlic*

The eels are fried in the oil and seasoned with salt and pepper. They are then covered with boiling water and allowed to cook for 15 minutes.

The almonds, parsley and garlic are ground down in a mortar, adding a little of the stock of the cooking. The mixture is added to the pan with the eel and cooked for a few minutes before serving.

For 6 persons. From the Restaurant Lara.

SARGO

GREY BREAM

The small ones are fried whole or simply sliced and fried. They are not very tasty.

They are best served stuffed with a cheese stuffing as for sardines (see page 131), and baked in the oven.

CHOPAS

BLACK-HEADED BREAM AND DORADAS (GILTHEAD)

Black-headed bream and doradas, which are like sargo but have a gold line across their heads, can be cooked in the same way as sargo.

ALBONDIGAS

FISH BALLS

For 1 lb white fish such as whiting or hake without the skin or bones, previously baked and flaked, the other ingredients are:

2 *eggs, beaten*	1 *tablespoon parsley*
1 *teacup breadcrumbs*	1 *clove of garlic, minced*
2 *tablespoons grated cheese*	*seasoning*

All the ingredients are mixed together and formed into balls about the size of a walnut, floured and fried in oil. They are then drained, covered with ½ pint tomato sauce and served.

For 6 persons.

GALLINA DEL MAR O CARPON

GURNARD

These fish are red with a large ugly head. They are delicious.

They are best served poached in the oven or baked in an oiled dish with butter and a little white wine and chopped parsley.

RUBIO

RED GURNARD

These are red fish with a big ugly head. They are not very good.

They can be fried whole or cooked in the oven on an oiled dish, sprinkled with a little chopped garlic, onion, parsley and tomatoes.

AJO HARINA (JAEN)

GARLIC FLOUR

1 *lb bacalao (dried cod which has been soaked overnight)*
2¼ *lb potatoes*
4 *tomatoes, skinned, seeded and finely chopped*
2 *sweet red peppers, finely chopped*
3 *cloves garlic, finely chopped*
½ *teaspoon saffron*
1 *tablespoon flour*
salt

The fish is cut into small pieces, fried in the oil, and removed to drain.

The potatoes are cut in thick slices and placed at the bottom of a shallow casserole. The fish is placed on the potatoes.

In the oil in which the fish was cooked, the chopped garlic, tomatoes and peppers are allowed to fry very slowly. When cooked, the saffron, flour and salt are mixed in and allowed to

cook, stirring well all the time. This sauce is then poured over
the fish in the casserole and the whole thing is simmered slowly
together either on the open fire or in the oven. Do not cover.

BACALAO EN AJO ARRIERO
(CASTILLA LA VIEJA)

2½ *lb bacalao, soaked overnight,*   2 *sweet red peppers*
  boned and cut into small pieces   2 *beaten eggs*
3 *cloves garlic*   *salt and pepper*
3 *tomatoes, skinned and chopped*   3 *tablespoons oil*

The garlic is fried in the oil until brown and then removed.
The tomatoes are then added to the pan and fried, then the
pimientos—which have been previously baked and skinned—
are added.

The bacalao is stirred in and the cooking is continued for a
few minutes over a low fire. The eggs are added and the pan is
stirred until the eggs are beginning to set. The dish is then
seasoned and served.

BACALAO A LA VIZCAINA (BASQUE)

DRIED COD À LA BASQUE

2½ *lb bacalao (dried cod)*   2 *large onions, sliced finely*
6 *sweet red peppers, roasted,*   ½ *pint oil*
  skinned and cut in thin slices   2½ *lb tomatoes, peeled, seeded and*
flour for coating   *quartered*
oil for frying

FOR THE PURÉE:

2 *cloves garlic*	2 *slices of bread fried and then*
½ *chopped onion*	*pounded in a mortar*
1 *lb coarsely chopped tomatoes*	*oil for frying*
6 *dried red peppers, soaked in*	*seasoning*
water	

The cod is cut in small equal pieces and soaked overnight in water. When required it is placed in cold water, which is allowed to come slowly to the boil. It is then drained well, skinned and boned. The pieces are floured and fried carefully in the oil. They are removed, drained, and kept in a warm place. In the same oil the onion is fried, the chopped tomatoes are added and this is allowed to cook slowly.

Purée (prepare before frying the bacalao). Chop the garlic, brown it in the oil and remove. Then allow the onion to soften in the oil without browning, add the tomatoes and red peppers and allow to cook slowly for about one hour, adding a little boiling water if necessary to keep the sauce from thickening too much. Then pass everything through a sieve and add the pounded breadcrumbs.

The purée is then mixed with the tomato and onion in the other pan. A layer of sauce is placed in an oven dish, the bacalao laid on it and covered with more sauce. This is repeated until the dish is full. Finally the pimientos are placed on top and the dish placed in a moderate oven for ten minutes.

BACALAO CON PATATAS (CADIZ)

DRIED COD WITH POTATOES

2¼ *lb bacalao*
2¼ *lb potatoes*
2 *large sliced onions*
3 *cloves garlic, sliced*
1 *bayleaf, powdered*
8 *sliced tomatoes*

2 *sliced sweet green peppers*
2 *sliced sweet red peppers*
12 *stoned olives, finely chopped*
salt and pepper
sufficient oil to cover

The bacalao is soaked overnight in cold water, then boned and cut in small pieces. The potatoes are sliced and a layer put in an oiled deep oven dish. A layer of fish is put on top. A little of all the remaining ingredients is placed on the fish and sprinkled with oil. The procedure is then repeated until the dish is filled, ending with a layer of potatoes. It is then cooked very slowly in the oven.

BACALAO DE ALCANTARA (ALCANTARA)

DRIED COD OF ALCANTARA

1 *lb dried cod*
1 *lb potatoes*
oil for frying

1 *finely chopped onion*
1 *lb spinach*
salt and pepper

The dried cod is soaked in water for 24 hours. It is then cut into small pieces, the bones removed and the pieces floured and browned in oil and then drained well.

The potatoes are sliced and browned slightly in the same oil with the chopped onion. Drain the potatoes and onion and completely cover the bottom of a flat oven dish with them. Then lay the dried cod on them and lastly the spinach, which has been previously cooked and well drained. Salt and pepper are sprinkled on and a glass of boiling water poured over. The dish is then put in the oven for about half an hour to finish cooking.

This is really a dish which is used for fast days. On other occasions, however, slices of bacon can be placed on the spinach.

BACALAO AL AJO ARRIERO (NAVARRE)

2¼ lb bacalao (dried cod)
2 cloves garlic
1 dessertspoon chopped parsley

1 teaspoon red pepper (paprika)
1 dessertspoon vinegar
salt

The bacalao is soaked overnight, cut in small pieces, floured and fried in oil. It is drained well and left in a warm place.

The garlic is fried in the same oil and then ground down in a mortar with the parsley and the salt. The red pepper and vinegar are mixed with the oil in the frying pan at the side of the fire. About 4 dessertspoons of water are mixed with the garlic and parsley paste and then added to the frying pan, mixed in well and poured over the fish, which is then reheated.

BUÑUELOS DE BACALAO

DRIED COD FRITTERS

These little fritters of dried cod are called 'tortillitas' in Andalusia.

½ *lb bacalao*
3 *tablespoons flour*
1 *tumbler milk*
3 *egg yolks, well beaten*

3 *egg whites, well beaten*
1 *teaspoon chopped parsley*
salt and pepper

The fish is soaked overnight. It is then cooked and the skin and bones removed. It is flaked as finely as possible. The milk is mixed with the flour and then stirred into the fish. It is seasoned and the parsley added. The yolks of egg are then mixed in and just before frying the stiffly beaten whites are folded in. The mixture is then fried in hot oil, a teaspoonful at a time.

MERLUZA

HAKE OR LING

Merluza can be prepared in the following ways:

Cut in steaks and fried, and served with chopped parsley.

Stuffed as for sardines.

Cut in steaks and placed on a buttered oven dish, sprinkled with salt, pepper and lemon and laid on finely chopped onion and parsley. Covered with buttered paper and baked.

Poached and allowed to cool, then served with mayonnaise.

Pastel de Merluza (Mould of Hake):

1 *lb hake*	3 *eggs, well beaten*
1 *tumbler tomato juice*	*seasoning*

Skin and bone the fish, flake it well, and mix with the tomato juice, eggs and seasoning. Put in a mould and cook in the oven. Turn out and serve cold with mayonnaise.

MERLUZA KOSKERA (CASTILLA LA VIEJA)

HAKE

¼ *lb hake cut in two steaks*	1 *clove garlic*
1 *hard-boiled egg*	*flour for coating*
2 *asparagus tips, boiled*	*salt*
a little dried crumbled chili	½ *teaspoon chopped parsley*
3 *dessertspoons oil*	*a few drops lemon juice*

The oil is heated in a pan and the garlic and chili fried in it. When it begins to brown, the floured hake is added. After two minutes about ½ tumbler of the asparagus water is added and it is cooked for a further 5 minutes, stirring from time to time. The hake is served with asparagus and sliced egg on top of it. It is sprinkled with the parsley, lemon and a little salt.

For 1 person. From the Restaurante Pinedo, Burgos.

CAZUELA DE MERLUZA A LA DONIASTIARRA (EL ESCORIAL)

CASSEROLE OF HAKE À LA DONIASTIARRA

This dish is typical of San Sebastian.

2 *onions, finely chopped*
2 *cloves garlic, finely chopped*
6 *hake steaks*
1 *tablespoon flour*
1 *small tumbler white wine*
4 *tablespoons oil*

12 *new potatoes, sliced and cooked*
1 *pint picked peas, cooked*
12 *asparagus heads, boiled*
4 *hard boiled eggs, quartered*
6 *small slices fried bread*

The onion and garlic are gently browned in oil in a casserole. The hake steaks are added and turned in the oil. The flour is mixed in and then the white wine. This is allowed to cook slowly for about 5 minutes, the steaks being turned from time to time. Just before serving, the potatoes, peas, asparagus and quartered eggs are added and mixed in the pan. A little crushed chili is mixed in and the fried bread added.

For 6 people. From the Hotel San Lorenzo.

CAZUELA DE MERLUZA VERDE MONTAÑESA (SANTANDER)

HAKE WITH GREEN SAUCE AND PEAS

This dish must be cooked in a casserole and not a saucepan.

1 *lb hake cut in 4 steaks*	*seasoning*
1 *finely chopped leek*	2 *tablespoons oil*
3 *finely chopped cloves of garlic*	1 *pint water*
1 *tablespoon parsley*	1 *breakfast cup of shelled peas*
1 *tablespoon flour*	

The chopped leek and garlic are gently browned in the oil, then the flour is stirred in and cooked slightly. The boiling water is now added, the sauce is stirred at the side of the fire, and then reheated and allowed to simmer for 15 minutes, with the parsley, seasoning and peas added.

The hake is now put in the casserole, the sauce and peas poured over it. It is cooked until the hake is tender, and served in the casserole.

For 4 persons. From the Restaurante las Caracoles.

MERLUZA MEUNIER A LA SERRANA (MADRID)

HAKE MEUNIER À LA SERRANA

4 hake steaks, floured
1 oz pork lard
2 oz lean ham chopped
2 cloves garlic, chopped very fine

1 dessertspoon chopped parsley
juice of 1 lemon
1 teacup meat stock

The steaks are fried slowly in the oil with the garlic, being turned so that both sides are browned. Then the parsley, juice of the lemon, ham and hot stock are added and the steaks cooked until tender. The steaks are removed, the sauce is reduced and poured over the fish.

For 4 persons. From the Hotel España, Guadalara.

MERLUZA EN SALSA (MADRID)

HAKE IN SAUCE

6 hake steaks
1 lb sliced potatoes

oil for frying

FOR THE SAUCE:

1 teacup chopped parsley
1 tablespoon flour
2 tablespoons oil
1 chopped clove garlic

1 chopped onion
seasoning
½ pint boiling water

The potatoes are sliced, fried in oil, removed and drained. The hake steaks are fried in the same oil. The potatoes are then placed in a flat casserole, the drained hake steaks are laid on the potatoes and the sauce is poured over them. They are allowed to cook slightly in the sauce.

To make the sauce. The oil is heated and a white roux is made with the flour, then the parsley, onion and garlic are mixed in and the boiling water is added to the pan at the side of the fire and stirred briskly. It is reheated and seasoned.

LAMPREA

LAMPREY

2 *lb lamprey*	*the livers of the fish*
1 *tumbler white wine*	*the blood of the fish*
1 *teacup oil*	*salt*
2 *onions*	

The lampreys must be washed in several changes of water and then cleaned, the blood being preserved. The heads are chopped off and the fish put in a casserole with salt to season, the white wine, oil, the whole onions and the liver. The pan is then covered and the fish stewed for two hours. The livers and onion are removed, mashed and strained and the blood is added. The sauce is then thickened with this mixture and the lamprey served in the casserole.

For 4–6 persons.

LISA

GREY MULLET

These can be cooked in a variety of ways:

Chopped in steaks and fried.

Baked whole in the oven, salted and peppered and sprinkled with white wine and oil.

Grilled and served with parsley sauce, etc.

Filleted and marinaded in oil and lemon juice, salted and then floured and fried.

SALMONETES

RED MULLET

The small red mullet can be fried whole. The larger ones can be placed in an oiled oven dish, sprinkled with lemon juice, salt and sherry, covered with buttered paper and baked in the oven.

SALMONETE AL HORNO

RED MULLET IN THE OVEN

2 lb red mullet	1 tablespoon chopped parsley
2 cloves garlic	1 wineglass white wine
1 tablespoon oil	2 tablespoons white breadcrumbs
juice of 1 lemon	1 nut butter

Clean and prepare your mullet. Oil a fireproof dish and lay the mullet in it. Cut the onion and garlic finely and place on the fish, salt and pepper it. Pour on the wine and lemon and finally sprinkle with the crumbs, dab on the butter and cover with buttered paper and place in the oven.

Before serving sprinkle with parsley.

PEZ DE LIMON

(SERIOLA DUMERILI)

This fish is known as 'Mediterranean Silver Fish' and is of the Carangoides family. It can be as long as from six to seven feet, and is silvery grey in colour with a yellowish iridescent streak running from head to tail on its flanks. It has a firm white flesh and is found on the coast of Morocco and the south of Spain. It is usually sold in steaks which are excellent poached or can be cooked in the same way as sole.

JURELES, BONITO, ETC

MACKEREL AND BONITO, ETC

The jurele most resemble the English mackerel although not of the Scomber family. The estornino (Spanish mackerel) and the jureles make good eating but the cavalla (mackerel) has dark red flesh and an unpleasantly strong flavour and is not good to eat. Jureles and estorninos, if small, can be fried or grilled. The best way of cooking the large mackerel is as follows:

Salt and pepper the fish. Put in a greased fireproof dish. Dab on small pieces of butter and cover with buttered paper. Cook in a moderate oven until the flesh is soft. Serve with Sauce Tartare or Salsa Verde (green sauce).

Bonito is of the mackerel family and makes excellent eating. It is best cooked like mackerel or can be cut in steaks and fried.

MERO

ROCK COD (EPHINEPHIUS GIGAS)

This fish is allied to the Serranus family. It may grow to six or seven feet in length. It has a firm white flesh. The small ones can be grilled whole or cut in steaks and fried, or used in fish soups, stews and rices. They make extremely good eating.

MERO

ROCK COD OR GROUPER

$2\frac{1}{4}$ *lb fish*
2 sliced onions
1 clove garlic
4 tomatoes, skinned and seeded
1 dessertspoon chopped parsley
a bouquet of herbs

$\frac{1}{2}$ *pint fish stock*
lemon juice
$\frac{1}{2}$ *tumbler white wine*
a few small sliced red peppers, if available

Remove the head from the fish and use it to make a fish stock.
Cook the onions in oil without browning, add the chopped

clove of garlic, the tomatoes quartered and the parsley, and simmer until soft. Then add the bouquet of herbs, the strained fish stock (or ½ pint water), a little lemon juice and half a tumbler of wine and simmer for about 15 minutes. Season.

Meanwhile salt and pepper the fish and lay it in a buttered fireproof oven dish. Pour the sauce over it, put two or three thin slices of lemon on the fish and two or three slices of tomato. Also, if available, the slices of red peppers. Cook it in a moderate oven for 35–45 minutes.

If preferred, before completely cooking, the fish can be skinned and filleted and returned to the dish.

RAPE

FROG FISH OR ANGLER FISH (LOPHIUS PISCATORIUS)

This fish is of the Lophides family. It has a flat body and is like a skate in appearance. It has an enormous mouth with sharp teeth and is greyish white in colour with brownish markings which become black on the tips of the fins. It is a solitary fish and is found in deep waters. It has a firm white flesh which is excellent for the table and tastes faintly like lobster. It is used for numerous soups and rices in Spain. It can be cut in steaks and fried, grilled, poached or cooked whole with lemon, tomatoes, green pepper, onion, etc, in a baking dish.

Rape is the *rana pescatrice* of the Italian Mediterranean coast, the *rospo* of the Adriatic.

RAPE EN CACEROLA (MALAGA)

ANGLER FISH IN CASSEROLE

2½ lb fish, cleaned and sliced
oil for frying
½ cup breadcrumbs

2 cloves garlic, finely chopped
1 tablespoon chopped parsley
salt and pepper

The fish is cleaned and sliced. The oil is heated with the garlic in it, the fish is then added and browned slightly on the outside. Then the breadcrumbs, parsley and lemon juice are added, the casserole is covered and the contents stewed slowly for half an hour.

RAPE AL HORNO (MALAGA)

BAKED ANGLER FISH

2¼ lb angler fish
1 chopped onion
2 tomatoes, peeled and seeded
12 almonds
12 monkey nuts
1 teacup breadcrumbs

3 cloves garlic
½ teaspoon saffron
1 teaspoon parsley
salt
oil for frying

The fish is cleaned and cut in thick slices. It is then placed in an oven dish and cooked in the oven for about ten minutes.

The almonds, nuts, garlic, parsley and breadcrumbs are all fried together in the oil and then pounded in a mortar to which is added the saffron.

The onion is chopped and fried and then the tomatoes are

added and allowed to simmer. The liquid from the fish is then mixed with the contents of the mortar and everything is then mixed with the tomatoes, seasoned, and poured over the fish, which is cooked for another ten minutes.

RATA DE MAR

URANOSCOPUS SCABER

This is an ugly fish with a large mouth. It is greyish brown in colour with a white belly and a black dorsal fin. It is about 15 inches long and lives in sandy depths of the sea but near to the coast. It is found on the Atlantic coast of Andalusia and in the Straits. It is only used in stews, rice dishes, etc, and does not make very good eating. In Italy it is called Pesce Prete.

RASCASCIO

ROCK COD

This fish is good baked simply in the oven. It is cleaned, salted and peppered, and placed in a buttered fireproof dish. It is sprinkled with chopped garlic, parsley, lemon juice and sherry, dabbed with butter and covered with buttered paper.

E

SALMON CON ACEITUNAS

SALMON WITH OLIVES

2 *lb salmon*	¼ *tumbler oil*
12 *green olives, stoned*	1 *tablespoon wine vinegar*
1 *tablespoon chopped parsley*	1 *nut butter*
1 *onion, chopped*	1 *hard-boiled egg, chopped*
2 *peppercorns*	*salt*

The salmon is placed in an earthenware casserole with the olives, salt, parsley, and peppercorns. The oil and vinegar are poured over it and butter dabbed on it. It is cooked in a slow oven and, when the salmon is soft, the hard-boiled egg is sprinkled on it and it is served in the casserole.

A Salsa Amarilla (see page 284) is served apart.

For 4–6 people.

SARDINAS

SARDINES

Sardinas Fritas—Fried Sardines. The most common way of serving sardines is simply to dip them in flour, cross the tails of three or four together and put them in oil and fry them. They are then taken out so that you get little bunches of about four sardines stuck together by their tails.

Sardinas Rebozadas—Sardines Fried in Batter. On other occasions they can be opened, and their bones, head and tail removed. The sardines are then dipped in a frying batter (which is made with the white of egg only) and then in boiling oil.

Sardinas Rellenas—Stuffed Sardines. One of the best ways to serve them is stuffed. They are split open, the bones, head and tail removed. A teaspoon of the following stuffing is spread on a fish and another sardine is placed on top and they are squashed firmly together. They are then floured and fried in hot oil.

Stuffing. Take 2 thick slices of bread about 3 inches square, remove the crusts and crumble the bread coarsely and leave it to soak in milk. You now need 2 tablespoons of grated cheese, 1 tablespoon chopped parsley, 1 grated clove of garlic and 1 well-beaten egg. When soft, squeeze out the breadcrumbs, and mash them with the parsley, garlic, and cheese; add the beaten egg and season with salt and pepper.

MORAGA DE SARDINAS A LA GRANADA (GRANADA)

1 *lb sardines*	1 *dessertspoon oil*
juice of half a lemon	3 *cloves chopped garlic*
½ *tumbler white wine*	1 *tablespoon chopped parsley*

The oil is heated and all the ingredients are added to it. They should be cooked from 10 to 15 minutes in a covered casserole on the fire and then served piping hot in the same dish.

SABALO (CADIZ)

SHAD

The fish is painted with oil and baked in the oven or on a grill. When the flesh is falling off the bones, the fish are taken out of the oven and left to cool.

They are then seized by the tail and all the scales are scraped off. They are boned and poached in water seasoned with salt and lemon juice.

SERRANO

SERRANUS SCRIBA

This fish is of the Serranus family. It is a rock fish and is related to the mero and the cabrilla. It is a very pretty fish, greyish in colour below but with a black stripe dorsally and vertical black lines going down from this stripe. Its body below the dorsal black line is a brilliant reddish orange colour which gradually merges with the silvery grey on the belly of the fish. Its flesh is white and good and it can be cooked like mero. Vaquito (or cabrilla) are similar in appearance, but tasteless.

RAYA EN PIMENTON (ANDALUCIA)

SKATE IN PIMENTON

2¼ *lb skate*
4 *cloves garlic*
1 *sprig parsley*
1 *teaspoon paprika*

1 *teaspoon saffron*
1 *teaspoon wild marjoram, finely chopped*

All ingredients except the fish are fried in oil, then ground down in a mortar. The skate is placed on an oiled oven dish, the mixture is sprinkled over it and it is cooked in the oven.

LENGUADOS

SOLE

Soles are fried as in England, sometimes simply floured and at other times egg-and-breadcrumbed.

FILETES DE LENGUADO (MADRID)

FILLETS OF SOLE

6 *fillets of sole*
1 *lb button mushrooms*
½ *tumbler white wine*

seasoning
¼ *lb butter*

The fillets are rolled and placed in a buttered dish. The mushrooms are stewed slightly in half the butter and then placed in the dish with the fish. The melted butter and liquid of the pan is poured over them. A little salt and pepper is sprinkled on the dish and the rest of the butter is dabbed on the fillets. The wine is added and the dish is cooked in a moderate oven.

LENGUADO A LA ANDALUZA
(ANDALUCIA)

SOLE À L'ANDALOUSE

1 *lb sole*
1 *breakfastcup rice*
oil for frying
1 *large onion, finely chopped*
1 *clove of garlic*
a pinch of saffron

2 *tomatoes, sliced*
2 *eggplants (aubergines), sliced*
4 *red peppers*
fish stock or water
parsley stuffing

The garlic is sautéd in oil until black, then removed. The onion is allowed to yellow slightly without browning in the oil and then the rice is added. It is allowed to absorb the oil and, when absorbed, boiling fish stock or water is added, from time to time, as necessary, together with a pinch of saffron and some salt.

The aubergines (eggplants) are finely sliced, dipped in flour and sautéd in oil. The tomatoes are cut in half and also sautéd in oil. The fillets of sole are filled with parsley stuffing (as for stuffed sardines, page 131), to which has been added one finely chopped red pepper. The amount of stuffing required is about half a teacup. The stuffing is spread on the sole fillets which are then rolled up, tied and poached in oil.

The remaining red peppers have their skins removed by heating them over the fire and are then sautéd in oil. Add to your rice the sole, the drained tomatoes, red peppers and aubergines.

LENGUADO A LA VASCA (NAVARRE)

SOLE À LA BASQUE

$2\frac{1}{4}$ *lb sole* $\frac{1}{2}$ *teaspoon oil*
1 *lb potatoes*   *juice of half a lemon*
1 *oz butter*   *salt*

FOR THE SAUCE:

1 *teaspoon chopped onion* $\frac{1}{2}$ *glass tomato juice*
1 *oz. butter*   1 *teaspoon cayenne pepper*
6 *small sliced mushrooms*   *salt*
2 *sweet red peppers, sliced*

The potatoes are sliced and put in a flat buttered dish in the oven—they should just cover the dish—and allowed to cook slightly. The cleaned fish are laid on the potatoes. They are sprinkled with salt and lemon juice and dabbed with the butter and oil. When cooked the liquid is strained off and the fish filleted.

The sauce is prepared separately. The onion is cooked gently in butter with the mushrooms and peppers. The tomato juice is added with the liquid from the fish and the sauce is seasoned.

The fish is placed in a buttered oven dish, covered with the sauce and heated for 10 minutes in a hot oven.

PEZ ESPADA O AGUJA PALADA

SWORD FISH

Fried. Allow ¼ lb per person and cut into fillets. Before cooking, season your fillets with salt and pepper and a squeeze of lemon. You can then fry the fillets after dipping them in flour or egg and breadcrumbs; or cut into smaller pieces and dip in French batter. They are good with a parsley sauce served separately.

Baked. Lay a piece of seasoned fish of about 1½ lb on a buttered fireproof dish. Sprinkle with sherry (about 1 tablespoon). Then chop fine one sweet red pepper, one tomato, one small onion and one teaspoonful of parsley. Place this mixture over the fish, dab with butter, cover with greaseproof paper and cook in a moderate oven.

When cooked remove the liquid which you find surrounding your fish. Make a Béchamel sauce using this liquid, which is made up to half a pint with milk, and poured over the fish.

Poached. First make your stock, using 1 quart of water, 2 tablespoons vinegar, 2 small carrots, 2 chopped onions, a bouquet of herbs, salt and pepper. Four peppercorns, if possible, should be added after half an hour. Cook this very slowly for one hour, then strain and allow to cool.

Just cover your fish with this and cook until soft.

Grilled. Cut the fish into very thin slices and marinade them for one hour with a chopped onion, 1 tablespoon chopped parsley, 2 cloves of garlic and sufficient oil just to cover them. Take them out, drain them, and then grill very slowly.

PEZ ESPADA EN AMARILLO (ANDALUCIA)

SWORDFISH IN AMARILLO

2¼ *lb swordfish cut in steaks*   1 *bayleaf*
5 *cloves garlic*   1 *teaspoon saffron*
1 *slice bread*   *oil for frying*
1 *sprig parsley*

The bread, garlic, parsley and bayleaf are fried together. When cooked the saffron is mixed in. This is all pounded together in a mortar and then ¾ of a pint of water is mixed with it. The fish is placed in an oiled oven dish, the sauce is poured on it and it is then cooked in the oven.

BAILA

SEA TROUT

These fish resemble the bass and the recipes for bass (see page 103) apply to it.

TRUCHA CON UNTO (LEON)

TROUT WITH LARD

The trout should be freshly caught, cleaned and stuffed with a little lard (clarified pork fat). It is then grilled and served.

TRUCHA (NAVARRE)

TROUT

The trout is marinaded in red wine, peppercorns, mint, thyme, rosemary, bayleaf, chopped onion and parsley for one hour. It is then cooked in this marinade.

It is served surrounded by boiled potatoes and carrots. The marinade is reduced and strained. The yolk of one egg per trout is beaten into it. It is heated until it thickens and then poured over the trout.

TRUCHAS FELIPE V (SEGOVIA)

TROUT PHILIP V

$\frac{1}{2}$ *lb fat bacon* $\frac{1}{4}$ *lb finely sliced ham*
1 *pint oil*   2 *lemons*
2 *cloves garlic, finely chopped*   6 *trout, of the same size*
2 *dessertspoons chopped parsley*

The trout are cleaned, washed and dried and seasoned with salt and pepper.

The oil and the fat bacon in one piece are placed together in a frying pan, and when the bacon fat is liquefied the trout are cooked in it, turning them two or three times so that they are evenly cooked.

They are then drained and placed on a dish. A little of the oil in which they have been fried is then used for frying the parsley and garlic. When they are well fried the ham is added and then the juice of the two lemons. This is heated and then poured over the trout.

The dish is decorated with vegetables, etc.

For 6 people. From the Restaurante Meson Candido.

TRUCHAS A LA JUDÌA
(ZAMORA, CASTILLA LA VIEJA)

TROUT IN THE JEWISH WAY

6 *trout*	1 *pint fish stock*
becollas (spring greens)	*salt and pepper*
2 *chopped cloves garlic*	*oil for frying*
1 *tablespoon flour*	1 *tablespoon chopped parsley*

The trout are cleaned. The becollas are fried in a saucepan with the garlic, then the flour is added and allowed to colour slightly. Half the fish stock is then mixed in.

The trout are placed in an oven dish, and the sauce is poured over them and enough stock is added to cover them. It is seasoned and the dish put in the oven and allowed to cook for half an hour. The trout are then drained well and placed in a dish. The sauce is reduced and strained over them and the parsley is sprinkled on them. They are served very cold.

RODABALLO

TURBOT

Turbot can be cut in steaks and fried or baked. They can be skinned and filleted, dipped in flour and beaten egg and fried. The large ones can be poached and served with sauce.

ATUN

TUNNY FISH

Fresh tunny fish is difficult to obtain but tinned tunny is plentiful. The recipes for swordfish also serve for tunny fish.

ARAÑA

WEAVER

These fish are not often caught because of their poisonous sting. They are the most lovely blue colour when fresh, going into almost a rainbow of colours. Their flesh is firm and white and they are good grilled or fried.

PESCADILLA

WHITING

This fish is more tasty than the English variety. They are never served with their tails in their mouths. They can be fried or cooked in a variety of ways.

PESCADILLA A LA PARILLA

GRILLED WHITING

The whiting are cleaned and the skin scraped; they are mari-

naded in oil, parsley, onions and shallots, salt and pepper. They
are left for an hour or so and then taken out and grilled. The
marinade is sprinkled on them from time to time.

CHANQUETES (MALAGA)

WHITEBAIT

Chanquetas are the equivalent of whitebait. They are found on
the coast of Spain near Malaga. Both are cooked in the same
way.

They are washed in cold water and dried, put on a floured
cloth or greaseproof paper, more flour is sprinkled on them
and they are well shaken. They are then fried in hot oil and
well drained. Repeat until all are fried. Do not cook too many
at once as they will not be floured or cooked evenly. Season
with pepper and salt, and serve quarters of lemon apart and
thin slices of brown bread and butter.

PESCADO BLANCO EN AJILLO
(ANDALUCIA)

WHITE FISH IN AJILLO

2¼ *lb skinned and filleted white*   2 *slices grated brown bread*
  fish such as whiting, pollack, 1 *dessertspoon oil*
  red gurnard or bass   *salt and pepper*
5 *cloves garlic, sliced fine*   *the juice of* 1 *lemon*

The garlic, breadcrumbs, oil, salt, pepper and lemon juice are mixed together. A layer of this mixture is put in an oiled deep oven dish, then fillets of fish, then more mixture until the dish is full. Sprinkle with oil and put in the oven.

PESCADO EN BLANCO A LA MALAGUEÑA (MALAGA)

WHITE FISH À LA MALAGUEÑA

1 *lb white fish such as whiting,*   1 *sprig parsley*
   'rape', bream, sole, etc   1 *bayleaf*
1 *chopped sweet green pepper*   2 *dessertspoons oil*
1 *chopped tomato*   *salt*
1 *chopped onion*   2 *pints cold water*
2 *chopped cloves garlic*

The fish is cut in thick slices and boiled. It is then removed from the water when nearly cooked and the water from the cooking is made up to 2 pints. All the other ingredients are boiled together until cooked. The fish is added at the last minute, the soup is skimmed well and served.

CALAMARES

SQUID

Calamares are small squid or inkfish. They are tasty when young and not tough like the cuttlefish (chocos or jibia). When small they can be cooked in a sauce made of their own ink, and when larger they can be stuffed.

CALAMARES EN SU TINTA

SQUID IN THEIR INK

The head and bag containing the ink are removed and the ink kept. The large spine is removed. The beards, antennae (the tentacles) and skin are finely chopped. These are then fried in oil. They are then removed and a teaspoon of chopped onion for each small inkfish is added to the oil. When cooked, a dessertspoon of flour is shaken in, cooked slightly, and about one tumbler of water added. The calamares are then added. A little of the liquid is mixed with the ink which is then poured over the calamares.

CALAMARES RELLENOS

STUFFED INKFISH

They are prepared as previously. One teaspoon chopped onion and one teaspoon chopped ham are allowed per fish and mixed with the chopped antennae. The sac is then filled with this mixture and the end is sealed by sticking a toothpick through it. After this they are fried in oil and then boiled with a little more chopped onion. A little tomato sauce may be added but it is better simply to add their own ink.

CHOCOS CON HABAS (CADIZ)

CUTTLEFISH WITH BROAD BEANS

4 *tablespoons oil for frying*   ½ *pint boiling water*
5 *cloves garlic*   *salt and pepper*
1 *lb cuttlefish*   1 *tablespoon chopped parsley*
1 *lb broad beans*

Put the oil in a deep pan, add the garlic and fry it. Prepare and chop the cuttlefish and add to the oil; allow to cook for about 10 minutes, stirring it all the time. Now add the broad beans and about ½ pint of boiling water. Cook until the beans are tender. Season, sprinkle with parsley, and serve.

CHIPIRONES EN SU TINTA (EL ESCORIAL)

SMALL INKFISH IN THEIR INK

10 *inkfish*   2 *cloves garlic, chopped fine*
2 *onions, chopped fine*

FOR THE SAUCE:

1 *large onion*   1 *bayleaf*
2 *cloves garlic*   ½ *cup oil*
2½ *lb tomatoes*   1 *small chili*
1 *sprig parsley*   *salt and pepper*

The inkfish are opened and the ink kept on one side. They are prepared in the usual way. The tentacles are chopped fine, mixed with the onions and garlic and fried in oil. The fish are then filled and the opening closed with a toothpick.

It is best to prepare the sauce first and leave it to cook as it must thicken, and should cook slowly for at least an hour.

The onion and garlic are chopped and cooked slowly in the oil without browning. The tomatoes are peeled, seeded and chopped; when the onion is soft they are added, together with a little chopped chili. They are seasoned with salt and pepper, the bayleaf and parsley are added and the pan is covered.

When the inkfish are ready, the ink is stirred into the tomato sauce, the inkfish are added and they are cooked in the sauce. They are served on little individual earthenware dishes and a white rice is served apart.

For 6 people. From the Hotel San Lorenzo.

ALMEJAS

COCKLES

These are small cockles. They must be well washed and then they can be fried with parsley and chopped onion in a little oil until they open. They are usually served with rice or in fish soup.

ALMEJAS A LA MARINERA (ANDALUCIA)

COCKLES À LA MARINERA

2 *to* 3 *pints cockles*　　　　　*oil for frying*
3 *cloves garlic, chopped*　　　1 *large onion, chopped*
1 *tablespoon chopped parsley*　½ *cup breadcrumbs*
1 *bayleaf*　　　　　　　　　*juice of half a lemon*
2 *wineglasses white wine*　　　*pepper and salt*

The cockles are well washed and placed in cold water to cover them and brought rapidly to the boil. The ones that do not open are lifted out and thrown away. The water is strained and kept aside.

The onion and garlic are slightly browned in the oil, the breadcrumbs are added and stirred round. Now add the water in which the cockles have been cooked, the wine, the crushed bayleaf, the lemon and pepper. The cockles are now added and allowed to cook a little. Season with salt and pepper, add the chopped parsley and serve.

COQUINES (CADIZ)

COCKLES

These are like almejas and are found at the mouth of the river. They can be cooked as for 'Almejas con Arroz' (page 159).

OSTION (CADIZ)

These are like small oysters but cannot be eaten raw. They can be egg-and-breadcrumbed and fried, or cooked in oil with breadcrumbs, parsley, garlic and pepper.

MOLUSCOS AL VAPOR (VALENCIA)

STEAMED SHELLFISH

The moluscos are cooked in a saucepan with a little oil, stirring constantly, for ten minutes. No salt or water should be added as they produce their own. They are simply seasoned with a little pepper, cinnamon and a few slices of lemon which are placed in the pan with them.

For 6 persons. From the Restaurant Lara.

LANGOSTA A LA CATALANA I
(BARCELONA)

CRAYFISH À LA CATALANA I

1 *medium-sized crayfish, cut in pieces*	½ *tumbler white wine*
oil for frying	2 *dessertspoons chopped parsley*
2 *tablespoons finely chopped onion*	½ *teaspoon saffron*
6 *tomatoes, peeled and seeded*	½ *teaspoon cayenne pepper*
2 *sweet red peppers, baked, skinned and cut in strips*	1 *tablespoon cognac*
	4 *small slices fried bread*

The crayfish (also called salt-water crayfish) is cut up alive and fried in the oil on a very hot fire, then taken out and drained. The onions are fried in the same oil, then the tomatoes and peppers are added and fried. The crayfish is then returned to the pan with the white wine, parsley and saffron and allowed to simmer for half an hour. The crayfish is removed and the sauce reduced on a hot fire.

The cognac is lighted in a warm soup-spoon and put into the sauce with the cayenne.

The crayfish is placed on a serving dish, the sauce poured over it and the dish surrounded by slices of fried bread.

If cooked crayfish is used for this dish it should be simmered for a little less time.

For 4 people.

LANGOSTA A LA CATALANA II
(LERIDA)

CRAYFISH À LA CATALANA II

1 crayfish of about 2¼ lb

The crayfish is split in half alive. It is seasoned with salt, black pepper and lemon juice, smeared with oil and grilled.

FOR THE SAUCE:

12 *almonds roasted in the oven*
2 *cloves of garlic*
½ *teaspoon black pepper*
½ *teaspoon red pepper*
1 *teaspoon parsley*

2 *tomatoes, skinned and seeded*
juice of 1 *lemon*
2 *tablespoons vinegar*
2 *coffeecups olive oil*

All ingredients are ground together in a mortar and served with the crayfish.

For 2 people. From the Hotel Palacio.

LANGOSTA AL ESTILO DE IBIZA (BALEARES)

CRAYFISH IBIZINCAN STYLE

10 *small calamares (inkfish) of
    equal size*
1 *rata de mar (see page 129),
    boiled, skinned, boned and
    mashed*
10 *mussels, cooked, shelled and
    chopped*
1 *hard-boiled egg*

*oil for frying
seasoning*
2 *cloves garlic*
2 *pints tomato juice*
1 *large live crayfish, preferably
    split in half before cooking*
1 *teacup Cazalla (a white,
    medium dry, local anis)*

The fish, mussels and hard-boiled egg are mixed together and used to stuff the inkfish, the ends of which are then folded over and sealed with a toothpick.

The oil is placed in a large pan on the fire and the garlic is browned and taken out. The tomato juice is now added and heated. The crayfish is then put in the tomato juice, together with the inkfish. They are allowed to cook fiercely for a few minutes, then the seasoning and wine are added. The pan is covered and the cooking completed on a low heat.

The crayfish is then placed on a dish surrounded by the inkfish, and the sauce is reduced and poured over the fish.

LANGOSTINAS A LA PLANCHA (CADIZ)

GRILLED DEEP-SEA PRAWNS

'Langostina' is a misleading name. Unlike the French 'langoustine', they do not resemble langouste (crawfish or salt-water crayfish). The crustacean which is called 'langoustine' in French is called 'cigala' in Spanish. The Spanish langostinas are outsize prawns with a dark red shell which has large black spots on it.

Langostinas must be well washed. They are then grilled on a hot iron plate, still in their shells, and served hot.

LANGOSTINAS A LA MARINA (CADIZ)

DEEP-SEA PRAWNS À LA MARINA

2¼ *lb langostinas*   1 *teaspoon black pepper*
5 *cloves garlic*   1 *glass wine*
1 *bayleaf*   *salt*
1 *onion*   ½ *pint boiling water*
2 *tablespoons chopped parsley*   *oil for frying*

The deep-sea prawns are washed well and shelled. The oil is heated in a saucepan and the garlic, onion, bayleaf and parsley, all chopped finely, are added. When nearly cooked, the pepper is added and the cooking continued. The prawns, white wine, water and salt are then put in, the pan covered with a close-fitting lid and cooked on a low fire for about 20 minutes.

LANGOSTINAS A LA VINAGRETA LEVANTINA (CASTELLON)

DEEP-SEA PRAWNS WITH EASTERN VINAIGRETTE

4½ *lb deep-sea prawns*
1 *teaspoon salt*
½ *teaspoon pepper*
2 *cups vinegar*
4 *cups oil*

2 *finely chopped hard-boiled eggs*
1 *finely chopped onion*
1 *pinch cayenne pepper*
½ *teaspoon saffron*
2 *wineglasses cognac*

The prawns are cooked in salted water and peeled. A vinaigrette is made with the salt, pepper, vinegar and oil; the other ingredients are mixed in, the cognac being added last.

The prawns are placed in a casserole, the sauce is poured over them and the casserole tightly covered.

They should be left for at least six hours before eating.

LANGOSTINA A LA ESPAÑOLA

DEEP-SEA PRAWNS À LA ESPAÑOLA

1 *breakfastcup langostinas without heads or skins*
1 *finely chopped clove garlic*
½ *bayleaf, chopped*

1 *teaspoon chopped parsley*
1 *small onion, chopped*
1 *sherry glass white wine*
oil for frying

The garlic, onion, bayleaf and parsley are fried slightly together in oil. The langostinas and white wine are then added and the pan covered and cooked slowly for 20 minutes.

CAMARONES O GAMBAROS (CADIZ)

SHRIMPS

The Spanish despise the humble shrimp, which is hardly ever used. The only current use is as a filling for omelettes.

RICE DISHES

RICE DISHES

El arroz, el pez y el pepino, nacen en agua y mueren en vino.
Rice, fish and cucumber, born in water and die in wine.

Rice is one of the national dishes of Spain. It is rarely simply boiled and only rarely seen as a sweet, i.e. milk with rice (see Desserts). Rice dishes vary considerably from the elaborate ones containing meat, chicken, fish, and many vegetables, to the simple peasant's midday meal which may consist only of vegetables and rice and perhaps a lump of tocino (fat bacon). Spanish rice recipes are many and varied, and are extremely tasty if well cooked; they are also very nourishing. Although in Spain the Spaniard usually uses fresh ingredients, in England one can make excellent Spanish rice supper dishes to use up meat, fish, etc, and with a little imagination one can turn out an excellent and satisfying meal.

Rice varies considerably, both as to the size of the grain and its hardness. Rice which is older and dried needs to be cooked for a longer time and more water or stock is required. It is always better to add your stock gradually and not all at once, as you may have far too much liquid and a sticky mess will result.

The method of cooking for all the given recipes is the same, but individuals differ as to the degree of dryness required of the rice. In the best cooking it should be moist rather than dry, but never overcooked and never running with water. The meat and vegetables are first cooked a little in the oil and the rice is then added and allowed to absorb the oil. Good clean fresh rice need not be washed first but shaken on a sieve and any impurities picked out. If dirty or old it should be washed in boiling water and then several cold waters, but it must be dried in the oven before being added to the oil. The rice must simply absorb the oil and must be on a low fire. It must never be allowed actually to fry as this makes the rice hard. When the rice grain becomes slightly transparent the hot water or stock is stirred in. It must then boil for about 5 minutes and simmer for 15–25 minutes according to the type of rice.

The Valencian rice is excellent for Spanish rice dishes. Fish should be cooked apart and added at the last minute, although the peasants fry meat and fish together. It is always better to dry off the rice slightly in the oven before serving.

The name 'paella' comes from the dish in which the rice is cooked and served. This is a flat oval pan with two handles. In some regions earthenware dishes are used, but this is not the classical manner. It is often cooked in a thick iron saucepan and then served on a china dish. When the boiling water is added some people add a few drops of lemon juice, which helps to separate the grains.

ARROZ ABANDA (VALENCIA)

RICE ABANDA

1 *lb rice*	3 *onions*
½ *lb rape (see page* 127)	3 *cloves garlic*
1 *lb cockles*	½ *teaspoon saffron*
¼ *lb weaver*	1 *bayleaf*
½ *lb rata de mar (see page* 129)	1 *teaspoon chopped parsley*
½ *lb cooked deep-sea prawns*	*salt and pepper*
½ *lb red gurnard*	*oil for frying*
3 *tomatoes*	

The fish is cleaned, the heads and tails are removed, and it is cut in fairly thick fillets. A stock is made by frying the chopped onion in the oil and then adding the chopped tomatoes, garlic, bayleaf and parsley and 4 pints of boiling water. This is seasoned with salt and allowed to simmer for a few minutes before the heads and tails of the fish are added. The stock is then simmered for half an hour and passed through a sieve.

The fish and shellfish are now cooked in the stock for about 15 minutes. The stock is then drained off; there should be about 2 pints—if not, a little water is added. When boiling, the rice and saffron are added and the boiling continued for about 15 minutes. The rice is then dried slightly in the oven. The fish and rice are served on separate dishes.

ALCOCHOFAS CON ARROZ

GREEN ARTICHOKE PAELLA

3 *green artichokes*	2 *cloves garlic*
1 *breakfastcup rice*	1 *packet saffron*
2 *tomatoes*	*oil for frying*
1 *onion*	

Prepare the artichokes by removing all the hard outer leaves and cutting off the stalks. Then cut off the tips of the leaves, not by cutting straight across but by cutting the outer layer lowest, the second layer a bit higher and so on until one is left with a core. The artichokes are then quartered lengthways and put to cook in boiling salted water.

Meanwhile the rice is thoroughly washed, first with boiling water to split the envelope of the grains and so release the starch, then repeatedly in cold water until the water is clear. It is dried in a cloth and then spread out on a dish in the oven to dry. If the rice is thus prepared it is never soggy and each grain is distinct.

Cover the bottom of a deep frying pan or wide saucepan with oil. Chop the garlic and onion and fry in the oil, then add your skinned, sliced tomatoes and allow to simmer for about 5 minutes. Now add your rice and allow to absorb all the oil, stirring all the time and not allowing it actually to fry.

Strain the artichokes from the water in which they have been cooked and gradually add this hot liquid to the rice, stirring well. Do not leave and do not pour on the stock and 'hope for the best'. Every rice is different and some requires more fluid than others. Stir constantly, adding more and more of the artichoke water as required. Also add the saffron and more salt and pepper.

The rice should boil for 5 minutes and simmer for 20, and should be ready for eating then. Add the artichokes and mix with the rice about 10 minutes before finishing. Dry off in the oven a few minutes before serving. Season as desired. This dish is made even prettier by adding a few slices of red peppers, which can be bought in jars or tins. The yellow rice, green artichokes and red peppers make a pleasing contrast.

ARROZ A LA ALICANTINA (ALICANTE)

RICE À LA ALICANTINA

2¼ *lb white fish*
12 *small French artichokes*
   (*young and whole*)
4 *sweet green peppers*
salt to flavour

oil for frying
2 *cloves garlic*
1½–2 *pints boiling fish stock or*
   water
½ *lb rice*

The procedure is the same as for all Spanish rice dishes. The fish is fried in the oil, which has previously been flavoured with the garlic. The rice is first cooked a little in this oil and the fish stock and seasoning added. The rice is decorated with the slices of fried fish and the artichokes (which have been boiled and drained) and the dish is reheated for about 5 minutes in the oven.

ALMEJAS CON ARROZ (ANDALUCIA)

COCKLES WITH RICE

3 *breakfastcups of cockles*
2 *onions*
4 *cloves garlic*
1 *tablespoon chopped parsley*

1 *teaspoon saffron*
2 *sweet red peppers*
2 *breakfastcups rice*
oil for frying

The cockles must be washed very well in several changes of water to get rid of the sand, and are left to soak in the last water. They are then placed in a saucepan with cold water and are brought to the boil until they open. Throw away those which do not open. Meanwhile fry the chopped onion and garlic in oil in another pan, then add the rice and the cockles, stirring all the time. When the oil has been absorbed by the rice, add the boiling water in which the almejas have been cooked and boil for 5 minutes, then simmer for 20 minutes. Add salt, pepper and the chopped parsley.

When cooked, decorate the dish with the red pepper which has been baked and skinned.

A refinement is to shell the cockles.

ARROZ CON ALMEJAS Y CALAMARES

RICE WITH COCKLES AND SMALL SQUIDS

2 *lb cockles*	1 *tomato, skinned and seeded*
1 *lb squid (inkfish)*	2 *large onions*
2 *large cups rice*	*oil for frying*
1 *large cup shelled peas*	3 *cloves garlic*
1 *teaspoon saffron*	*salt and pepper*

The cockles are cooked and shelled. The squid are cleaned and chopped as for Calamares Fritos (page 143). The procedure is the same as for cockles with rice. The onion and garlic are cooked in the oil and the chopped tomato added, then the rice, stock, fish and saffron, followed by the peas, previously boiled.

POLLO CON ARROZ

CHICKEN WITH RICE

1 *chicken of about* 3 *lb*   *salt*
1 *quart stock* $\frac{1}{2}$ *lb rice*
2 *tablespoons chopped parsley*

The chicken is cleaned and then put in boiling stock made
from the giblets, which must be sufficient to cover it. It is
flavoured with salt and parsley and simmered for about an hour
or until tender.

The rice is well washed in boiling water and then cold. The
stock is strained off from the chicken through a damp cloth.
The rice is cooked slowly in the stock for 20 minutes to half
an hour, stirring all the time and allowing the rice to absorb
the stock. The chicken is then served surrounded by the rice.

ARROZ A LA MARINERA

RICE À LA MARINERA

24 *deep-sea prawns*   1 *cup shelled peas, par-boiled*
1 *lb hake*   24 *tips of wild asparagus*
2 *lb cockles*   4 *cloves garlic*
$\frac{1}{2}$ *lb inkfish*   2 *tablespoons chopped parsley*
1 *onion*   1 *teaspoon powdered saffron*
2 *tomatoes, skinned and seeded*   *salt and pepper*
2 *sweet red peppers*   *oil for frying*
2 *sweet green peppers*

F

The fish is washed, cleaned and cut in small pieces. The prawns are shelled and the inkfish prepared and cut up as for frying. The cockles are boiled and the shells removed. The water from their cooking is strained and saved.

In a deep frying pan put oil, the chopped onion and garlic, and fry until slightly brown. Then add the fish, chopped tomatoes, prawns, cockles, peas and the inkfish. Allow to simmer slowly until the peas and inkfish are cooked. The rice is then added and allowed to absorb the liquid. Shake the pan so that it does not stick. The water from the cockles is then added (this must be boiling) and then the saffron, pepper and salt. The rice is allowed to boil for 5 minutes, then it is simmered on a slow fire for about 15 minutes, adding more boiling water as required. It is then sprinkled with the parsley, decorated with strips of red and green peppers—which have been baked in the oven and skinned—and the boiled asparagus tips. It is placed in the oven for a few minutes before serving.

ARROZ CON MEJILLONES (LUGO)

RICE WITH MUSSELS

2 *cloves garlic, chopped*
1 *dessertspoon chopped parsley*
1 *teaspoon powdered saffron*
2 *doz. mussels, cooked and shelled*

¾ *lb rice*
salt and pepper
oil for cooking

FOR STOCK:

1 *cod's head*
1 *onion*
2 *young carrots*

2 *pints water*
salt

The garlic, parsley and saffron are pounded together in a mortar. The oil is heated in the casserole, then mixed with the paste in the mortar, and the mussels are added.

The stock prepared from the cod's head is strained in. When it begins to boil the flesh from the cod's head is added with the rice and seasoning. It should be kept boiling for 5 minutes and must be stirred constantly. It is then simmered for another 10 minutes. The cooking is finished in the oven.

For 6 people.

PAELLA DE MARISCOS (VALENCIA)
A RICE AND SHELLFISH DISH

1 *medium-sized crayfish cooked and cut in pieces*	2 *cloves garlic*
	1 *chopped onion*
6 *cigalas (langoustines in French)*	½ *lb rice*
1 *lb rape (see page* 127*) cut in pieces*	1 *teaspoon red pepper*
	1 *teaspoon saffron*
6 *small inkfish*	*fish stock*
4 *tomatoes, skinned and seeded*	*oil for frying*

The fish are fried in oil with the garlic; when nearly cooked the onions are added, then the tomatoes. The rice is then stirred in and the oil absorbed slightly before adding enough boiling stock to cover the rice. Season with salt, pepper and saffron, and simmer until the rice is cooked.

For 6 persons. From the Restaurant Lara

PAELLA BRUTA (ALICANTE)

A ROUGH RICE DISH

3 onions
2 cloves garlic
1 breakfastcup rice
oil for frying
hot stock
2 chopped tomatoes
salt

saffron
1 lb pork cut in pieces
3 lb chicken, disjointed
1 lb white fish such as bass,
    whiting, etc
chicken stock

The garlic is fried in the oil and removed. The onions are added, then the chicken and pork are fried and removed. The fish is cut in thick slices and fried apart in different oil.

The rice is put into the pan with the oil and onions, and when the oil has been absorbed, boiling stock made from the giblets of the chicken is poured over, stirring all the time. To this are added 2 chopped tomatoes, saffron and salt. When the rice is cooked, the fish, meat and chicken are added and the dish is placed in a moderate oven for 5–10 minutes.

PAELLA A LA CAMPINA

A COUNTRY PAELLA

In this dish everything is cooked together and not previously fried.

½ *lb sliced ham*
1 *chicken of about 3 lb, dis-*
  jointed
¼ *lb chorizo (garlic sausage)*
small singing birds
2 *cloves*

½ *teaspoon pepper*
1 *bayleaf*
3 *cloves garlic, previously baked*
  in oven
½ *lb rice*
2 *quarts water or stock*

All ingredients are placed in a deep saucepan and stewed together, stirring from time to time to keep the rice from sticking, and adding more stock as required. When nearly cooked, do not add more water but allow to evaporate and finish off by drying in the oven.

This is a typical peasant dish, but the rice is frequently overcooked. I suggest that it is preferable to roast, fry or simmer the chicken a little before the other ingredients are added.

ARROZ A LA PEIZXATOR (ALICANTE)

RICE À LA PEIZXATOR

1 *large crayfish (about 2 lb)*
   which is sliced alive
4 *large fillets of sole*
   (about 1 lb)
1 *gurnard*
4 *sweet red peppers*
4 *tomatoes*

1 *cup shelled cooked peas*
6 *small green artichokes,*
   cooked
oil for frying
1 *breakfastcup rice*
1 *pint fish stock or water*

The crayfish is supposed to be cut up alive, but this seems exceedingly barbaric and most people will prefer to use a cooked crayfish.

The garlic is fried and then removed from the oil; and in the same oil the crayfish and other fish cut in pieces are browned and then removed. The chopped tomatoes and peppers are now fried in the oil, the rice is added and allowed to absorb the oil.

About a pint of boiling water or fish stock is then poured in, the rice is boiled for about 5 minutes and then simmered for about 15 minutes. After the first 5 minutes the crayfish is added, and just before the end, the gurnard and the sole. The dish must be stirred constantly and more liquid added as necessary. The peas and artichokes, previously boiled, are added at the last minute. A few more red peppers, fried apart, can be added for decoration.

ARROZ A LA VALENCIANA (VALENCIA)

RICE À LA VALENCIANA

The most famous Spanish rice dish cooked in a paellera (see page 156) is Arroz a la Valenciana. For this you need:

3–4 *lb chicken suitable for frying*	¼ *lb lean ham*
2 *cloves garlic*	1 *small garlic sausage, sliced*
2 *large onions*	1 *teacup shelled peas*
1 *tablespoon chopped parsley*	1 *teacup shelled cooked butter*
4 *sweet red peppers*	*beans*
4 *tomatoes*	8 *teacups rice*
½ *lb steak*	1 *small packet of saffron*
1 *small lobster*	*salt and pepper*
1 *dozen mussels*	

One finds that quantities vary from recipe to recipe according to individual taste. Sometimes a few green artichokes and asparagus are added. Small pieces of fried hake are also sometimes included. A small packet of saffron and salt and pepper are essential.

Cover the bottom of your pan with oil into which you put the two chopped cloves of garlic. When hot, you add the chopped onion and half the red peppers. When the onions are soft you add the tomatoes, sliced.

In this mixture you now carefully brown the chicken, cut up into small pieces complete with bones, together with the steak which has also been cut into small squares, and the small pieces of ham.

When the chicken is brown you add the garlic sausage, sliced, and to this you now add the rice. The rice is allowed to simmer in the oil. Shake it from time to time to prevent catching, but do not stir. When the rice becomes transparent, sufficient boiling stock to cover it is poured in, and salt, pepper and saffron are added. The rice should then be allowed to boil for 5 minutes and to simmer for 15. From time to time add stock as necessary to prevent catching. Again, it can be moved about but should not be stirred, as that would break up the grains.

The lobster, mussels and hake are cooked separately, as are also the remaining red peppers, the peas, and the butter beans. All are added to the dish just before serving. The dish is finally heated for a few minutes in the oven.

ARROZ CON LANGOSTINOS O GAMBAS

RICE WITH PRAWNS

2 *breakfastcups peeled prawns*
2 *large cups rice*
3 *tomatoes*
5 *cloves garlic*
2 *onions*

oil for frying
1 *teaspoon red pepper* (*paprika*)
salt and pepper
boiling water

Deep-sea prawns or ordinary prawns can be used. The chopped garlic and onions are fried in the oil without browning. The tomatoes are peeled, seeded and quartered, then added and allowed to cook for a few minutes. The rice is then put in and, when the oil is absorbed, boiling water is added, together with the salt, pepper, red pepper and the prawns. The cooking is finished as for Cockles with Rice (page 159).

ARROZ A LA ZAMORANA
(CASTILLA LA VIEJA)

RICE À LA ZAMORANA

¼ *lb lard*
1 *lb onions, sliced*
2 *small turnips (they have small round tender turnips in Spain)*
1 *tablespoon chopped parsley*
1 *teaspoon thyme*
1 *teaspoon wild marjoram*
3 *cloves garlic*
½ *teaspoon paprika*

1 *pig's foot, boned and cut in small pieces*
1 *pig's ear, boned and cut in small pieces*
1 *pig's chap, boned and cut in small pieces*
½ *lb finely chopped ham*
1 *breakfastcup rice*
6 *thin slices bacon*

The lard is melted in a deep pan and the onions and turnips are cooked in it without browning. When half cooked, the parsley, thyme, wild marjoram, garlic and paprika are added. This mixture must cook slowly until the onions begin to brown; it is then allowed to cook on a very low fire for 4 hours. At the end of this time 2 pints of boiling water are added and the ear, foot and cheek of pig and the chopped ham as well.

When the liquid is bubbling, the rice is added and for 10 minutes it is boiled vigorously, being well stirred, and more water being added if necessary. Then at the side of the fire the slices of lean bacon are laid on top of the contents of the dish and the dish is placed below a hot grill or in a hot oven until the bacon is cooked.

MEAT

MEAT

'Vaca' literally means cow, 'toro' bull and 'buey' bullock. 'Carne de vaca' is generic for beef, and carne de vaca is not usually good in Spain. It is old and tough. It is better to ask for veal (ternera), which is not young white veal, as in France, but resembles our own beef, as the calf is allowed to grow almost to maturity. Never eat beef when there has been a bull-fight, as one is probably eating the toro! Beef, when used, is better marinaded (adobado) first and then fried and stewed or simply stewed. Hanging of meat is not known; it is usually killed and eaten fresh. The origin of this is partly climatic and partly the result of lack of refrigeration.

In the north of Spain there are lovely lambs and sheep, but in the south, owing to climatic and nutritional conditions, the sheep are few and far between and poor in quality. Suckling lamb (lechon) is delicious in the north, as is the sucking pig (cochinillo or toston), which we find roasted in central Spain.

Generally in Spain meat is fried, and there are certainly excellent veal fillets. Roasting is not common except in the centre of Spain.

The Spaniards say that their climate is like their cooking; in the north they stew, in the centre they roast, and in the south they fry—and it is roughly true.

The 'cocido' is a stew of meat and vegetables. The liquid is strained off and used for soup, and the meat and vegetables are eaten as a second course, but the meat is usually overcooked, most of the goodness having gone into the soup. Other words for stew are found, such as 'calderada', 'calderete', etc, originating from the word 'caldera' (cauldron), i.e. the vessel in which the stew is cooked. 'Pote' (pot) is another word which originates in the same way.

173

MEAT: BEEF

Mas vale dos bocados de vaca que siete de patatas.
Better two mouthfuls of beef than seven of potatoes.

LOMO DE TORO

BEEF FILLET

2 lb fillet of beef

The fillet is cut into thin steaks and left to marinade for 6 hours
in the following mixture:

1 *teaspoon salt*	1 *tumbler white vinegar*
4 *cloves garlic*	½ *tumbler oil*

It should be covered and turned from time to time in the
marinade. It is then taken out, wiped dry, and fried in butter
or oil.

CADERO DE TORO

TOPSIDE OF BEEF

2 *lb beef*	1 *bayleaf*
6 *cloves garlic*	1 *tumbler oil*
1 *large onion*	1 *tumbler white wine*
2 *cloves*	2 *tumblers water*
6 *peppercorns*	1 *dessertspoon vinegar*

This is all heated slowly in an earthenware casserole for 4 hours.

The meat is taken out and drained. The sauce is strained and is thickened with 1 tablespoon of chocolate powder.

ESTOFADO DE VACA ESPAÑOLA (MADRID)

BEEF STEW

2 *lb good beef*	½ *teaspoon curry powder*
2 *oz bacon*	1 *teaspoon parsley*
1 *large onion, sliced*	2 *lb new potatoes*
3 *cloves garlic, chopped*	2 *tablespoons oil*
1 *teaspoon mixed herbs*	1 *tumbler white wine*
½ *teaspoon red pepper* (*paprika*)	1 *wineglass vinegar*
3 *tomatoes, skinned, seeded and*	1 *tumbler stock*
chopped	*salt*

The beef and bacon are cut in small pieces. The garlic and onion are placed in a stewing pan with the meat and bacon, covered with the oil, white wine and vinegar, placed on a very low fire and allowed to cook for ten minutes, stirring occasionally. Herbs, curry, red pepper and the tomatoes are added, then the tumbler of hot stock. Cook slowly and when tender add the peeled potatoes and continue cooking until these are cooked. Before serving sprinkle with parsley. Approximate cooking time is 2 hours, but this of course depends upon the cut and quality of the meat.

For 4 people. From the Palace Hotel.

CAZUELA A LA CATALANA (LERIDA)

MINCED BEEF

2 *lb minced beef*
½ *lb butifarra (sausage, see*
   page 42), *sliced*
oil for frying

2 *chopped onions*
2 *chopped tomatoes*
2 *chopped carrots*
1 *tablespoon flour*

A flat earthenware dish must be used and the bottom covered with oil. The meat is fried in this and then removed.

In the same oil the carrots, onions and tomatoes are fried together, stirring well to prevent sticking. The flour is then stirred in and allowed to cook a little. Then the meat is stirred in and a little hot stock or water is poured in and it is left on a low fire to cook for about 45 minutes, care being taken that it does not get too dry.

When the meat is tender the slices of butifarra are placed round the edge of the dish and it is heated in a hot oven.

For 6 people.

LENGUA A LA ARAGONESA (ARAGON)

TONGUE À LA ARAGON

1 *cow's tongue*—1½ *lb to 2 lb*
2 *sweet green peppers*
2 *carrots*
1 *large onion*
1 *head of garlic*
3 *tomatoes*

1 *sprig parsley*
1 *sprig thyme*
1 *clove*
1 *tablespoon grated chocolate*
salt and pepper
oil for frying

The tongue is washed and cooked for ten minutes in boiling water. It is allowed to cool and is then scraped. The oil is heated in a saucepan and the tongue gently heated in it, turning from time to time.

All the other ingredients are then added, together with a little more oil and the pan is covered and allowed to simmer for 3 hours.

The tongue is drained, placed on a dish and cut in slices. It is surrounded by sliced boiled carrots and the sauce of the cooking is strained and poured over it.

ESTOFADO DE VACA O TERNERO (ARAGON)

CASSEROLE OF BEEF OR VEAL

2 *lb meat*
¼ *tumbler oil*
2 *large onions*
4 *cloves garlic*
1 *bayleaf*
1 *sprig thyme*
1 *large carrot*

1 *tomato*
1 *sweet green pepper*
1 *tumbler white wine*
salt
1 *lb potatoes can be added if
    required*

A piece of lean meat should be chosen. The meat is placed in a casserole with the oil and garlic and allowed to brown gently. The chopped onions and sliced carrot are then added, together with the chopped green pepper and the sliced tomato. These are allowed to fry for a few minutes, then the wine is added and allowed to boil. Sufficient boiling water is added just to cover the meat. The stew is seasoned with salt and the bayleaf and thyme are added. The casserole is now tightly covered and allowed to simmer slowly for 3 hours.

The potatoes, sliced or whole if small, can be added after 2 hours. It should be served in the casserole.

For 4 persons.

MORROS DE TERNERA A LA VIZCAINA (BASQUE)

CALF'S CHEEKS IN THE BASQUE WAY

2½ lb calf's cheeks (morros de ternera)
4 chopped onions (about 1 lb)
6 dried red peppers
4 finely chopped cloves garlic
1 tablespoon chopped parsley
1 wineglass oil
1 dessertspoon flour
salt and black pepper for seasoning
½ pint boiling stock

The calf's cheeks are well washed in cold water, which is changed three or four times; they are also well scraped. They are then placed in a saucepan and covered with cold water. Whilst they are cooking the sauce is prepared as follows:

The onion, garlic and parsley are cooked slowly in the oil; when the onion is soft the flour is stirred in and allowed to cook without browning; the boiling stock is added to the pan at the side of the fire, is well beaten and then returned to the fire. It is allowed to boil slowly for two or three minutes, being beaten with a wooden spoon all the time, then it is put on the side of the fire and seasoned with salt and pepper.

The peppers are washed, placed in cold water and brought to the boil. When soft they are drained and then scraped, the soft interior being added to the sauce, and the skin being ground down in a mortar, mixed with a little water. This is then stirred into the sauce.

The sauce is again brought to the boil and then rubbed through a fine sieve. The morros are cut into small equal-sized pieces, placed in a thick pan, and the sauce poured over them. They are then simmered for about half an hour, stirring from time to time. They should be served in the pan in which they are cooked.

PERDICES DE CAPELLAN (MALLORCA)

CHAPLAIN PARTRIDGES

This recipe does not contain partridges at all but thin slices of veal steak. For each person 2 thin slices of veal are required, weighing about 2 oz each.

6 *slices good veal*	3 *cloves garlic*
6 *slices ham*	1 *teaspoon mixed herbs*
6 *slices sobresada* (*a form of*	*salt and pepper*
pork sausage)	1 *wineglass white wine*
oil for frying	½ *pint boiling stock*
butter	

The slices of veal are well beaten. They are each covered with a slice of ham and a thin slice of the pork sausage. They are then rolled up and tied, or fastened with a toothpick.

They are floured, and fried in a mixture of oil and butter with 3 cloves of garlic and a teaspoon of mixed herbs, salt and pepper. When browned evenly a wineglass of white wine is added and half a pint of boiling stock; the pan is covered and they are allowed to simmer for about 30 minutes. The sauce should be very reduced.

For 3 persons.

TERNERA A LA SEVILLANA (SEVILLE)
VEAL À LA SEVILLANA

1 *lb veal*	1 *wineglass sherry*
oil for cooking	12 *olives*
1 *dessertspoon flour*	2 *medium-sized carrots*
1 *onion*	1 *teaspoon parsley*
2 *cloves garlic*	*salt and pepper*
1 *pint stock*	

Sufficient oil to cover the bottom is put in a deep saucepan. The garlic is browned in the oil and then removed. The veal is browned in the oil and drained, then the onion and carrots are sliced, browned in the same oil and drained. The flour is added to the oil, stirred well and cooked slightly. The boiling stock is then added, stirring all the time. Lastly the sherry goes into the pot.

The veal and vegetables are then replaced, seasoning and parsley added, the saucepan is covered and allowed to simmer slowly until the veal is cooked (about 1 hour).

When the veal is cooked the sauce is passed through a sieve and the veal is reheated in the sauce together with the olives which have been previously stoned.

TERNERO CON ALCACHOFAS A LA CORDOBESA (CORDOBA)

VEAL WITH GLOBE ARTICHOKES À LA CORDOBESA

2¼ *lb lean veal*
8 *artichokes*
2 *oz beef dripping*
1 *breakfastcup stock*

2 *large onions*
½ *glass wine of Montilla*
salt and pepper

Remove the outer leaves and the stalks of the artichokes, then cut the tops of the remaining leaves. The prepared artichokes are then par-boiled in boiling salted water, then strained. The fat is melted in a deep saucepan or fireproof dish and in this the meat and sliced onions are browned. The excess fat is drained off and the artichokes are added together with the stock, wine, salt and pepper. The pan is covered and allowed to cook slowly for about 2 hours.

Instead of artichokes, peas or a tomato sauce can be used.

TERNERA ASADA

ROAST VEAL

2¼ *lb veal*
¼ *lb butter*
        or
2 *tablespoons oil*

salt and pepper
1 *glass white wine*
1 *onion, finely chopped*

The meat is browned in the oil or butter in a saucepan or casserole; it is then seasoned, the wine and onion are added, the

pan covered, and it is allowed to cook very slowly for 2 hours.
It is served surrounded by a purée of potatoes.

ESCALOPES DE TERNERA LABRADOR (MADRID)

ESCALOPES OF VEAL LABRADOR

6 *thin slices of veal, about*
    4 inches by 2 inches
12 *thin slices of ham, about*
    4 inches by 2 inches

flour for coating
1 *beaten egg*
breadcrumbs

The slices of veal are sandwiched between the ham and kept
together by means of a toothpick. They are floured, dipped in
beaten egg and breadcrumbs and then fried in lard. The tooth-
picks are removed before serving.

For 6 people. From the Hotel España, Guadalara.

MENUDO GITANO O CALLOS A LA ANDALUZ

TRIPE À LA ANDALUZ

3¼ *lb veal tripe*
3 *calves' feet*
½ *cup vinegar*
juice of 1 *lemon*
1 *lb chick-peas*
1 *chopped onion*
1 *ham bone*
10 *cloves garlic*
1 *dessertspoon paprika*
2 *chopped carrots*
1 *dessertspoon mint*

½ *lb chorizo (garlic sausage)*
¼ *lb morcilla (blood sausage)*
salt
bayleaf
parsley
2 *skinned sweet green peppers,*
  chopped and fried in oil together
  with 2 tomatoes, 1 onion, ¼ lb
  ham, ½ teaspoon nutmeg powder
  and ½ teaspoon powdered saffron

The tripe is placed on the table and well scraped with a knife. When clean it is cut into 2-inch squares. The calves' feet are halved and then divided into small pieces. The tripe and calves' feet are then placed in a bowl with salt, the lemon juice, half a cup of vinegar and water sufficient to cover the tripe. It is then washed in a fresh supply and the water changed 5 or 6 times until it remains clean. The tripe and feet are then placed in a saucepan and covered with cold water, which is brought to the boil and then strained off.

The chick-peas—which have been soaked overnight, the chopped onion, ham bone, chopped cloves of garlic, paprika, chopped carrots, salt, mint, parsley and bayleaf are put in a pan with the tripe and feet and covered by about 1¾ pints of water. This is allowed to boil on a low fire till tender. Then the chorizo and morcilla are added and it is left to cook slowly.

The onion, green peppers and tomatoes (skinned, seeded and fried together in oil) are then poured over the tripe.

The stew is served in a casserole, the chorizo and morcilla sliced and placed on top of the tripe, and sprinkled with saffron and nutmeg.

CALLOS A LA MADRILEÑA (MADRID)

TRIPE À LA MADRILEÑA

1 *lb veal tripe*	½ *tumbler white wine*
2 *lb calf's foot*	1 *wineglass Spanish brandy*
1 *lemon*	2 *dried red peppers*
1 *teaspoon chopped parsley*	1 *chili*
½ *teaspoon chopped thyme*	1 *onion*
1 *bayleaf*	2 *oz chopped lean ham*
salt	2 *oz sliced chorizo*
3 *peppercorns*	1 *dessertspoon flour*

The tripe must be cleaned very carefully. It must be scraped with a knife, cut in small pieces and washed in various changes of water. It is then placed in white wine with salt and a lemon quartered and scrubbed until white and clean.

The calf's foot must also be washed and the flesh removed from the bone.

The tripe and calf's foot are then placed in a saucepan with the parsley, thyme, bayleaf, salt and peppercorns and brought slowly to the boil. The water is then strained off and fresh water added so that it just covers the meat. The wine, cognac, dried peppers and the chili are also added. When cooked, the onion is chopped, fried and mixed into the saucepan, together with the ham and chorizo. The sauce is thickened with the flour and reheated.

HIGADO A LA ASTURIANA (ASTURIAS)

LIVER À LA ASTURIANA

2½ *lb liver (calf's or sheep's) sliced and cut in small pieces*
2 *oz fat bacon*
2 *oz butter*
4 *onions (medium sized), finely chopped*

4 *tomatoes, peeled and seeded*
12 *almonds, peeled*
½ *tumbler white wine*
1 *clove garlic*
salt and pepper

The bacon is slowly fried in the butter in a saucepan, then the liver is added with the chopped onion. These are allowed to cook for a few minutes, then the tomatoes and wine are added, the dish is seasoned, covered, and slowly stewed for an hour. The almonds and garlic are pounded together in a mortar, gradually adding about a cupful of water. After half an hour this is added to the saucepan. The liver is placed on a dish and surrounded by small triangles of toasted bread.

SESOS FRITOS

FRIED BRAINS

The brain of a calf is cleaned, the skin and veins removed. It is well washed, and boiled in water containing vinegar in the proportion of 1 dessertspoon to a pint, with one onion and salt, for about 30 minutes. It is then taken out, drained, and carefully dried. It is cut into small pieces, floured, dipped in beaten egg and fried in very hot oil.

As an alternative it can be dipped in batter to which a little aguadiente has been added, and then fried.

MEAT: LAMB

Carnero comer de caballero.
Lamb is food for gentlemen.

CORDERO LECHAL EN CHILINDRON

SUCKING LAMB IN CHILINDRON

See Pollo en Chilindron, page 212.

The method of cooking a young sucking lamb is the same as for cooking chickens 'En Chilindron'. For a sucking lamb of 3 lb one needs the same quantities as for 3 chickens.

CHULETAS DE CORDERO A LA NAVARRA (NAVARRA)

LAMB CHOPS À LA NAVARRA

6 *lamb chops*
2 *oz ham cut in small pieces*
1 *large onion, chopped*
6 *tomatoes, seeded, peeled and chopped*

¼ *lb chorizo (sausage) of Pamplona cut in fine slices*
salt
equal parts of lard and oil for frying—about 1½ *oz of each*

The lamb chops are browned on both sides in the fat and oil mixture and removed. In the same fat the chopped ham is fried with the onion, and when slightly browned, the tomatoes are added and cooked until a thick sauce is formed. This is seasoned and then poured over the chops in an oven dish. The chorizo is placed on the chops and it is heated in the oven until slightly soft and then served in the same dish.

CALDERETE DE CORDERO (JEREZ)

LAMB STEW

This is a delicious stew made with lamb less than a year old, allowing half a lamb per person.
For each 2¼ lb lamb one needs:

4 *cloves garlic*
4 *tablespoons oil*
2 *large sliced onions*
salt and pepper
1 *dessertspoon flour*

1 *glass boiling water*
4 *peppercorns*
1 *dessertspoon finely chopped mint*
wine vinegar

The lamb is disjointed and is allowed to marinade for one hour in equal parts of water and wine vinegar. It is then drained, washed in clean running water and dried well.

The oil is heated in a large saucepan, the cloves of garlic are browned in it, then removed and kept. The meat is then added and carefully browned in the oil, then the sliced onions are added, together with the flour which is well stirred until the oil is absorbed. This must simmer over a low fire, then the boiling water is added, the pan is covered and the lamb is slowly cooked.

Meanwhile the fried garlic is pounded in a mortar with the peppercorns, the mint and a little salt. A little of the sauce of the cooking is mixed with this and then all is added to the pan. The meat is removed and the sauce reduced. It is then poured over the meat and served.

CORDERO EN AJILLO PASTOR (JAEN)

The name of this dish indicates that it is a shepherd's dish, i.e. a very simple method of cooking used in country kitchens.

1 *sucking lamb*	1 *tablespoon flour*
1 *tablespoon paprika*	1 *lb fried potatoes*
6 *cloves garlic*	*oil for frying*
1 *teaspoon powdered saffron*	*salt*
1 *tumbler white wine*	

The sucking lamb is cut in small pieces and slowly browned in oil until tender. The paprika is then stirred in. The garlic and saffron are ground together in a mortar and then added. The flour is stirred in and, when bubbling, the wine is added, together with the salt. The dish is covered and allowed to cook slowly for 15 minutes. It is served surrounded by the fried potatoes.

CORDERO ASADO (LOGROÑO)

ROAST LAMB

A joint of lamb of about 2 lb is cut in small slices, salted and peppered, smeared with good pork lard and put in a hot oven in a casserole where it is allowed to cook slowly.

When browned, half a tumbler of wine is poured over it, then it is sprinkled with lemon juice and served.

COCHIFRITO (NAVARRA)

FRICASSEE OF LAMB

2¼ *lb lamb*
1 *large onion, chopped*
3 *cloves garlic*
1 *teaspoon paprika*

6 *peppercorns*
1 *tablespoon chopped parsley*
juice of half a lemon
oil for frying

The lamb is cut in small pieces. The garlic is browned in the oil and then the lamb added and browned carefully on both sides. The chopped onion is then added. The paprika is stirred in with the parsley, lemon juice and salt. The pan is covered and allowed to simmer until the lamb is tender.

CORDERO LECHAL ASADO ALCARREÑO (MADRID)

ROAST SUCKING LAMB ALCARREÑO

The lamb must only be a few days old. It is cleaned, cut in half, rubbed with salt and good pork fat. It is roasted in a casserole —not a saucepan or tin pan—with one bayleaf, a sprig of thyme and 2 or 3 thin slices of lemon on top. It should be roasted in a hot oven.

From the Hotel España, Guadalara.

CORDERO ASADO ESTILO BURGOS (CASTILLA LA VIEJA)

ROAST LAMB IN THE STYLE OF BURGOS

a lamb weighing 10 *lb*　　　　　*salt*
½ *lb good pork lard*

The lamb is divided in two, and salted. The lard is melted in a baking tin and the lamb is placed in with the back uppermost. The oven must be very hot and the lamb basted from time to time.

This is served with potatoes and salad.

For 8 persons. From the Restaurante Pinedo, Burgos.

CHULETAS A LA PARRILLA CON ALI-OLI

LAMB CHOPS GRILLED WITH ALI-OLI

These are grilled lamb chops served with ali-oli, the mayonnaise with garlic (page 279).

RIÑONES DE CORDERO A LA SEÑORITA

LAMBS' KIDNEYS À LA SEÑORITA

6 *lambs' kidneys*
1 *onion*
2 *slices ham*
½ *pint Sauce Espagnole*
   (*page* 279)
1 *hard-boiled egg*

2 *cups shelled peas*
1 *cup white wine*
12 *mushrooms* (*if possible*)
parsley
salt and pepper
fried bread

Cut the kidneys in thin slices. Butter a deep frying pan and put in the kidneys, seasoning, finely chopped onion and finely chopped parsley and cook quickly for 3 or 4 minutes in the wine.

Cook the peas and mushrooms. Add these and the Sauce Espagnole to the pan and cook slowly until the kidneys are tender.

Serve on a large dish garnished with the ham, chopped hard-boiled egg and fried bread.

RIÑONES AL JEREZ

KIDNEYS IN SHERRY

6 *sheep's kidneys (or 4 pigs')*	2 *tablespoons good stock*
oil for frying	1 *dessertspoon flour*
½ *tumbler sherry*	1 *teaspoon chopped parsley*
1 *egg of butter*	*salt and pepper*

The kidneys are skinned, cleaned, fried in hot oil and then sliced. They are put in a casserole and cooked in the sherry for 2 minutes.

A roux is made with the butter and flour and the stock is added, seasoned and the parsley stirred in. This is then poured over the kidneys and they are served immediately.

MEAT: PORK

Carne hace carne y vino hace sangre.
Flesh makes flesh and wine makes blood.

COCHINILLO ASADO DEL MESON DE SEGOVIANO (MADRID)

ROAST SUCKING PIG I

The pig must be 21 days old. It is washed and the skin well scraped. It is split from the mouth to the tail, cleaned and well washed. It is then placed in a large pan with the belly uppermost. It is sprinkled with about 1 tablespoonful salt, 2 bayleaves are placed on it, and a layer of butter—about 2 oz. The cooking is then commenced in a hot oven and after a few minutes 3 cloves of garlic crushed in the mortar with a little wild marjoram are sprinkled over it. After three-quarters of an hour it is turned and the skin is pricked to let some of the fat escape. It has to be left in the oven for about another three quarters of an hour, when the skin will be brown and crisp.

COCHINILLO ASADO (SEGOVIA)

ROAST SUCKING PIG II

The sucking pig should weigh between 2–3 kilos (2¼ lb to a kilo). It is seasoned with salt, grated garlic and white pepper. The pig is split straight down from the skull to the tail through the spine. It is then placed in a meat pan on its back. A little wine and water should cover the bottom of the pan and one or two bayleaves are added. It is then placed in a hot oven and when brown on the underside it is turned and pierced with a fork and then baked with lard until well browned. The only sauce served is the juice of the cooking.

For 6 people. From the Restaurante Meson Càndido.

G

LOMO DE CERDO A LA ARAGONESA
(ARAGON)

LOIN OF PORK À LA ARAGONESA

loin of pork of about 2 lb
salt
flour for coating
oil for frying
1 onion, sliced
4 cloves garlic, chopped

4 tomatoes
1 tumbler white wine
½ teaspoon cinnamon
2 hard-boiled eggs, finely chopped
1 teaspoon finely chopped parsley

The loin of pork is sliced, salted, peppered and floured. It is then fried in the oil and when browned on both sides it is removed. The garlic and onion are then fried in the same oil and when soft the tomatoes—peeled and seeded—are added. The meat is placed in a casserole and the sauce, to which the wine is added, is poured over the meat, which is sprinkled with cinnamon, and the cooking is finished in the oven. Before serving, in the same dish, it is sprinkled with the finely chopped hard-boiled eggs and the parsley.

Author's Note. This is the refined version. In the original everything is fried together and the wine is added and simmered. The cinnamon is not used but about 6 stoned black olives can be added at the last minute, together with the sliced egg.

From the Hotel Palacio, Madrid.

JAMON CON HABAS A LA GRANADINA
(GRANADA)

HAM WITH BROAD BEANS

2¼ *lb broad beans*   ½ *lb ham*

It is very important that the beans are tender and fresh and the ham should be Serrano, from Alpujarro.

The beans are shelled and tossed in hot fat, stirred constantly. The ham is cut in slices, about ½ centimetre thick, and is mixed with the beans and heated just before serving.

Ham Serrano is the delicious dried ham one finds in the south of Spain.

From the Hotel Victoria.

MANITOS DE CÉRDO REHOGADAS
(VALLADOLID)

FRIED PIG'S FEET

The feet are cleaned and boiled. When cooked the bones are removed, if possible without destroying the shape of the feet. They are then floured, egg-and-breadcrumbed and fried in oil.

RECHO DE CERDO A LA PAISANA
(LA CORUÑA, GALICIA)

PIG'S STOMACH IN A PEASANT WAY

In Galicia a pig's stomach is called a recho. The stomach is well scraped and washed in several changes of salt water and lemon juice. It is then stuffed with lean cooked pork cut up fine, together with a little chorizo. The recho is sewn up and boiled for an hour and a half. It is left to get cold and then cut in thin slices and used as an hors-d'œuvre.

SALCHICHA EXTREMEÑA

EXTREMEÑA SAUSAGE

Equal parts in weight of lean meat, liver and tocino (fat bacon) are put on a low fire, together with wild marjoram and anis to taste. When evenly browned it is minced and well mixed, then placed in a narrow intestine. It is then cooked in a bain-marie.

Tocino, in Spain, is the skin and fat from any part of the pig. All joints have the skin and fat removed before they are sold, and crackling is unknown.

CACHELADA (LEON)

This is a dish of potatoes and chorizo (garlic sausage). The chorizo is placed in a pan, just covered with water and slowly heated. When boiling, peeled quartered potatoes are added. When the potatoes are cooked the liquid is drained off and the

potatoes and chorizo are served together. The water in which
they are cooked is used for vegetable soup.

LACON CON GRELOS (LEON)

SHOULDER OF SALTED PORK AND WHITE CABBAGE HEART

The pork is boiled until it is falling off the bone, then the cabbage hearts are added and cooked until tender. The meat and
cabbage are drained and served together.

CALDERETE EXTREMADURA DE CABRITA (EXTREMADURA)

EXTREMENEAN STEW OF KID

5 *cloves garlic*	*cayenne pepper*
oil for frying	2 *sweet red peppers*
1 *small kid*	1 *bayleaf*
the kid's liver	1 *glass red wine of Extremadura*

The cloves of garlic are fried in the oil in a deep pan, then
removed. In the same oil the disjointed kid is browned and
when brown is removed and drained. In the same oil the kid's
liver is fried with red pepper cut in pieces. The peppers,
liver and garlic are then pounded in a mortar. Everything is
replaced in the oil and the glass of wine and a bayleaf are
added, together with about half a pint of boiling water, some
salt and the cayenne. It is then all stewed together slowly until
the kid is tender. The kid is then removed. The sauce is
reduced, if necessary, skimmed, then poured over the kid.
   Lamb can be cooked in the same way.

MEAT: MISCELLANEOUS

La olla y la mujer reposadas han de ser.
A stew must be cooked slowly and a woman must be tranquil.

COCIDO MADRILEÑO

MADRID STEW

½ *lb garbanzos (chick-peas)*
  soaked for 12 *hours*
1 *lb shoulder of beef*
2 *lb boiling fowl*
¼ *lb bacon*
¼ *lb ham*
1 *chorizo (garlic sausage)*
1 *morcilla (blood sausage)*
1 *salted pig's foot, soaked for*
  12 *hours*

6 *pints water*
½ *green cabbage or spinach*
1 *onion*
1 *leek*
1 *carrot*
1 *lb small new potatoes*
2 *tablespoons rice or* 2 *oz*
  vermicelli

FOR SMALL BALLS:

2 *oz minced beef mixed with*
2 *tablespoons breadcrumbs*
½ *teaspoon mixed spice*

1 *beaten egg*
salt and pepper

A large deep stewing pan is required for this dish. The chick-peas and salted pig's foot are soaked overnight. The meat, bacon, fowl and ham are placed in the pan, together with the water. It is heated slowly and constantly skimmed. When boiling, the chick-peas, pig's foot and the small balls are added.

The stew is brought to the boil again, seasoned, the onion added and it is cooked very slowly for 3–4 hours.

The chopped leek, carrot and cabbage are boiled in another pan with the chorizo and morcilla. About 15 minutes before the stew is finished the potatoes are added to the vegetables, etc.

When ready, the liquid is strained off from the meat and the vermicelli or rice is heated in it, and this forms the soup.

The meat is removed from the stew, sliced, and placed in the centre of the dish with the chick-peas surrounding it.

The vegetables are drained and heated again in a frying pan in a little oil with a crushed clove of garlic.

The morcilla and chorizo are sliced and placed in another dish surrounded by the potatoes and vegetables.

A thick purée of tomatoes can be served with this dish, which is an elaborate form of Cocido. It can all be cooked in one pan, adding the vegetables and morcilla after the meat has been cooking for about 2 hours.

POTE GALLEGO (ORENSE)

GALICIAN STEW

1 *lb steak, cut in large pieces*	2 *oz lean bacon, chopped*
¼ *lb lean ham, chopped*	1 *lb dried haricot beans*
¼ *lb morcilla (blood sausage), sliced*	1 *white cabbage, chopped*
¼ *lb chorizo, sliced*	2 *lb potatoes*

The meat is covered with 2 pints of cold water, seasoned, and allowed to cook on a slow fire. In another saucepan the haricot beans and white cabbage are cooked until tender, then added to the saucepan with the meat; at the same time the potatoes are added and allowed to boil. When the potatoes are cooked, the stock is strained off and used as a soup. The vegetables and meat are served separately.

GUISADO DE TRIGO
(ALBACETE, LA MANCHA)

STEW OF WHEAT

6 *wheat cobs*
½ *lb chick-peas, soaked overnight*
1 *pig's foot*
¼ *tumbler oil*
2 *chopped tomatoes*

2 *sweet red peppers, sliced*
2 *onions, finely chopped*
2 *cloves garlic, chopped*
salt and pepper
1 *teaspoon mint*

The wheat has the outer leaves, etc, removed, and the cobs are then placed in a deep saucepan of boiling water, together with the pig's foot and chick-peas. The water should only just cover them and they are allowed to boil vigorously and then more cold water is added until the grains of the wheat burst open. The centre core is then removed. It is then simmered until the chick-peas are tender and most of the water is absorbed. The tomatoes, peppers, onion and garlic are simmered in the oil until there is a thick sauce. This is then mixed in with the stew and it is seasoned and allowed to cook slowly for another five minutes. Just before serving it is sprinkled with the chopped mint.

ALBONDIGAS

MEAT BALLS

1 *teacup chopped ham and veal*   1 *dessertspoon chopped parsley*
1 *tablespoon chopped onion*   2 *beaten eggs*
1 *small chopped slice chorizo*   *seasoning*
   (*garlic sausage*)

Everything is mixed well together and formed into tiny balls about the size of a walnut. They are dipped in flour and beaten egg and fried in deep oil or butter. They are then drained and placed in a casserole and over them is poured either a tomato or almond sauce (pages 284 and 280).

PASTEL DE MURCIA (MURCIA)

MURCIAN PASTY

A pastry case is made and in this are placed pieces of veal, chorizo (garlic sausage), hard-boiled eggs, brains and minced meat, with a little stock to moisten. The tart is then covered with circles of very light puff pastry and cooked in the oven.

MORCILLA BLANCA O RELLENOS A LA NAVARRA

WHITE SAUSAGE À LA NAVARRA

12 *beaten eggs*
½ *lb boiled rice*
6 *oz chopped suet*
1 *tablespoon chopped parsley*
1 *chopped onion*

2 *chopped cloves garlic*
½ *teaspoon cinnamon*
1 *teaspoon saffron*
salt
small intestines for filling

The eggs are beaten and mixed with the boiled rice, chopped suet, parsley, onion, garlic, cinnamon and saffron and seasoned with salt. The intestines are well cleaned and loosely filled with the stuffing. The ends are tied and the sausages placed in hot water, having been pricked first to allow the air to escape. They are cooked on a low fire for about 40 minutes.

When cold they are sliced and fried with onions and covered with tomato sauce.

The sauce is made with 2 large, sliced onions, stewed in oil, and 1 pint tomato purée seasoned with salt and pepper, and cooked slowly for about 1 hour.

CHANFAINA (LEON)

This is a stew consisting of the legs of a kid, with the head, lungs and liver, plus green artichokes, silver beet, lettuce and peas. A somewhat specialized taste.

EMPANADAS DE BATALLON (LEON)

These are pasties filled with chopped ham, chorizo (garlic sausage) and red peppers, slightly flavoured with onion.

HORNAZO
(SALAMANCA—CASTILLA LA VIEJA)

This is a tart or pastry which is served on the Monday following Easter Monday.

A pastry is made, using $\frac{1}{2}$ lb flour, $\frac{1}{4}$ lb butter, 1 egg, and water to mix.

FOR THE FILLING YOU NEED:

2 oz sliced chorizo   *2 sliced hard-boiled eggs*
2 oz chopped ham   *salt and pepper*
any cooked pieces of chicken,   *a little stock to moisten*
  turkey, etc

This is made in the form of a Cornish pasty and like this is taken into the country for picnics and eaten cold.

COCIDO ANDALUZ

ANDALUSIAN STEW

½ lb chick-peas, soaked overnight	½ lb morcilla (red sausage)
1 lb lean beef	3 cloves garlic
¼ lb piece of fat bacon	½ teaspoon saffron
2 long bones of beef, broken	½ teaspoon pimentòn (paprika
1 rib bone of beef, without meat	powder)
1 lb large French beans	salt and pepper
1 lb potatoes	½ lb spaghetti or vermicelli
1 slice pumpkin	1 wineglass red wine
½ lb chorizo (garlic sausage)	1 tomato, peeled and seeded

The meat, rib bones, bacon, etc, are well washed and put to boil in 4 pints of water with salt and pepper. When boiling, the saucepan is put on the side of the fire to simmer slowly, skimming as required.

The beans are prepared and put in boiling salted water with the chick-peas; when par-boiled they are drained and added to the saucepan with the meat, the potatoes, pumpkin, chorizo and morcilla. When cooked, the stock is drained off, skimmed well and boiled, the spaghetti being cooked in the boiling stock, which makes the soup.

The meat, bacon, chorizo, morcilla, etc, are sliced and placed on a serving dish with the vegetables. Over them is poured the following sauce:

The cloves of garlic are pounded in a mortar with the salt, pepper, saffron and paprika. The pumpkin is drained well and added, together with the tomato, and pounded to a paste. The wine is mixed in at the end and it is then reheated and poured over the meat and served.

POULTRY AND GAME

La gallina hace la cocina.
The chicken is the foundation of a good meal.

GALLINA EN PEPITORIA (MADRID)

CHICKEN IN PEPITORIA

1 *hen of about 4 lb*	1 *sprig thyme*
2 *cloves garlic*	12 *finely chopped almonds*
1 *sliced onion*	½ *teaspoon saffron*
2 *wineglasses good white wine*	2 *chopped hard-boiled eggs*
1 *tablespoon flour*	½ *cup fried breadcrumbs*
1 *pint hot stock*	1 *dessertspoon chopped parsley*
salt and pepper	*oil for frying*
1 *bayleaf*	

The hen is disjointed and fried in the oil but not allowed to brown excessively. The garlic and onion are then added and cooked lightly, then the white wine is poured in and allowed to reduce slightly. The flour is stirred in, then about 1 pint of hot stock, which should be just enough to cover the meat, and the bayleaf and thyme. Now cover the pan and cook slowly. After half an hour add the almonds and saffron and continue the cooking until the hen is tender. When serving sprinkle with chopped hard-boiled egg, the crumbs and parsley.

From the Palace Hotel.

PUCHERO DE GALLINA (MADRID)

STEWED FOWL

1 *boiling fowl of about* 4 *lb*	1 *turnip*
(*cleaned*)	3 *cloves garlic*
the liver of the fowl	*salt and pepper*
1 *leek*	*sufficient water to cover the fowl*
1 *carrot*	1 *dessertspoon flour*

FOR THE STUFFING:

1 *breakfastcup crumbs*	1 *egg butter*
2 *grated cloves of garlic*	2 *beaten eggs*
1 *tablespoon chopped parsley*	*salt and pepper*
1 *teaspoon chopped marjoram*	

The crumbs, garlic and herbs, salt and pepper are mixed together and the butter is then stirred in. Finally the beaten eggs are added and the hen is stuffed with this mixture. The fowl is stewed with the vegetables, garlic, salt and pepper until tender. It is then taken out of the stock, drained, cut into slices, and kept hot on a serving dish.

The fowl's liver is fried in oil, rubbed through a sieve and mixed with the flour. The stock is strained, reheated and reduced, and then gradually mixed in with the liver-flour mixture and reheated in the saucepan. It is then poured over the fowl.

POLLO A LA MANCHEGA (LA MANCHA)
CHICKEN À LA MANCHEGA

3½ lb chicken, which must be
   young and tender
2 oz butter
¼ tumbler oil
1 large onion
6 stoned green olives
3 chopped carrots, young and
   medium sized

1 tablespoon chopped parsley
3 cloves garlic, chopped
½ a small green cabbage, chopped
2 small chopped turnips
salt and pepper
1 teaspoon paprika
1 wineglass white wine
½ tumbler stock

The chicken is disjointed and is then browned in the oil and
butter, taken out and drained. The onion, parsley and garlic
are browned slightly, then the chicken is added to the saucepan
with the olives and carrots and allowed to simmer gently for
about ten minutes. The cabbage, turnips, wine, seasoning and
stock are then added. The saucepan is again covered and simmered gently for one hour.

POLLO EN SALSA DE VINO
CHICKEN IN WINE SAUCE

1 chicken
1 onion
saffron
1 clove garlic
2 sweet red peppers
flour
nutmeg

bouquet of herbs
2 cups shelled peas
2 tablespoons oil
fried bread
2 glasses white wine
potatoes

Disjoint the fowl and fry in oil in a large deep pan with the bouquet of herbs, chopped onion and garlic. Turn and brown (this takes about half an hour). Then sprinkle flour on the chicken. When it is brown add the wine and simmer. Lastly add the saffron and nutmeg.

Put the chicken on a hot dish. Skim the sauce and pour it over the fowl. Garnish with cooked peas, fried red peppers, fried bread and small potatoes cooked in oil or fat.

MENESTRA DE POLLO BILBAINA (EL ESCORIAL)

CHICKEN STEW WITH MIXED VEGETABLES

1 *good roasting chicken of about* 3 *lb*	2 *oz chopped ham*
oil for frying	2 *sliced carrots*
1 *cup picked peas*	2 *tablespoons flour*
12 *small new potatoes*	½ *tumbler white wine*
12 *asparagus tips*	1 *tumbler hot stock*
6 *green artichokes, quartered*	*salt and pepper*

The fowl is disjointed and placed in a little oil in a casserole, which is covered and placed over a very low fire so that the fowl does not brown and the juice which comes out of it is white. When there is sufficient juice, all the vegetables are added and are allowed to 'sweat' in the casserole, so that the flavour of the fowl enters into them. When they have been 'sweating' for about half an hour, the flour is stirred in and allowed to colour slightly. Then the white wine, hot stock and seasoning are added and the cooking continued on a low fire for another half hour or until the chicken is very tender.

From the Hotel San Lorenzo.

GALLINA EN PEBRE
(CASTILLA LA VIEJA)

CHICKEN IN GARLIC SAUCE

1 fowl weighing about 3½ lb

FOR BASTING FOWL:

6 oz butter
salt

3 cloves garlic
juice of 1 lemon

1 tablespoon chopped parsley
salt and pepper
1 bayleaf

1 wineglass oil
yolk of 1 egg

4 oz of the butter are mixed with the cloves of garlic, salt and lemon juice—which have been pounded together in a mortar. The chicken is then spread with this paste and put in the oven to roast. It is frequently basted and when brown but not cooked through, it is taken out of the oven.

The remaining butter, parsley and the oil are then heated in a large casserole or saucepan. The chicken is placed in this and the liquid from the roasting pan is poured over it. It is seasoned with salt and pepper and about ½ pint of hot stock is added. The casserole or saucepan is then covered and the chicken cooked slowly until tender. It is then placed on a dish, the sauce is thickened with the yolk of an egg, passed through a sieve and poured over the hen.

POLLO CHILINDRON (ARAGON)

CHILINDRON CHICKEN

In Aragon this is served as the one and only dish and one allows half a chicken per person, but the chickens must be young and tender and of at least 2½ lb.

3 chickens, cleaned and disjointed	1 large onion, chopped
2 cloves garlic, chopped	1 teaspoon parsley, chopped
12 dessertspoons oil	6 large red sweet peppers
salt and pepper	9 tomatoes, without skin or
¾ lb lean ham cut in thin slices	seeds

A tomato sauce is made by cooking one of the chopped cloves of garlic and the onion slowly in the oil without allowing them to brown. The tomatoes are then added and the sauce is allowed to simmer slowly for one hour.

The disjointed chickens are lightly browned in the oil containing the other chopped clove of garlic. They are then sprinkled with salt and pepper and the ham is added. When completely browned, the tomato sauce and chopped red peppers are stirred in, and the chopped parsley. The pan is then covered and allowed to simmer slowly until the chickens are cooked.

For 6 persons.

FRITO DE PECHUGAS DE POLLO (CORDOBA)

FRIED CHICKEN BREASTS

2 *chicken breasts*   *breadcrumbs*
1 *beaten egg*   *oil for frying*
flour

The breasts are each cut into two or three long strips. They are
then dipped in flour, egg-and-breadcrumbed and fried.

GALLINA RELLENA (CORDOBA)

STUFFED FOWL

1 *fowl, 3–4 lb*   2 *onions*
½ *lb chopped ham*   2 *leeks*
½ *lb fillet of veal*   2 *carrots*
salt and pepper   2 *dessertspoons chopped parsley*
½ *teaspoon powdered nutmeg*   1 *teaspoon chopped thyme*
½ *glass sherry*

The chicken is cleaned and then with great care it is skinned
whole. The flesh is then removed from the carcass and finely
chopped.

The chopped meats are mixed with the salt, pepper, nutmeg
and sherry and left to stand for 2 hours. The skin is then filled
with the stuffing, the chicken is reformed and sewn. It is then
wrapped in a clean cloth. The bones are placed in a stew pot
with the onions, leeks, carrots, herbs and the giblets. The

chicken is added and just covered with water. The pan is covered and the chicken cooked slowly for about 2 hours. It is then removed, drained and pressed well.

It is served sliced, with the sauce reduced and strained.

POLLO A LA CACEROLA ESPAÑOLA

SPANISH CHICKEN IN CASSEROLE

1 *chicken*	2 *slices chopped ham*
1 *onion*	1 *glass sherry*
6 *artichoke hearts*	1 *large cup tomato sauce*
potatoes	*bouquet of herbs*
2 *tablespoons oil*	*stock*

Chop the ham and onion finely and brown in a little oil. Disjoint the chicken and add to this, together with the bouquet of herbs and seasoning. When brown add the sherry, tomato sauce and a little stock (sufficient to cover the chicken) and stir well. Put on the lid and simmer. Fry the potatoes. Cook the artichoke hearts in butter.

Serve the chicken covered with the sauce and surrounded by the artichokes and potatoes.

FRITOS

This is a good dish for an informal supper. Chicken and ham are minced together.

4 oz chicken	1 breakfastcup milk
4 oz ham	2 oz butter
1 teaspoon flour	

A roux is made with the flour and butter. The warmed milk is
added and the sauce carefully stirred on the side of the fire.
The ham and chicken are then cooked slowly in this and
seasoned with salt. When a fairly solid paste is formed a sand-
wich is made with stale bread and firmly pressed together. It is
then painted with beaten egg, sprinkled with breadcrumbs and
fried in very hot oil.

PEPITORIA DE GALLINA O POLLO

STEW OF HEN OR CHICKEN

For a bird of about 3 lb when plucked and drawn the other
ingredients are:

2 medium-sized onions, sliced	salt and pepper
4 cloves garlic, sliced	¼ lb almonds, peeled
1 tablespoon chopped parsley	½ tumbler white wine
¼ lb butter	yolk of 1 egg
giblets	

The bird is cleaned and disjointed. The garlic and onion are
browned in the butter, then removed and kept hot. In the same
butter the disjointed bird is fried and, when brown, is sprinkled
with parsley.

The giblets are meanwhile stewed in 1 pint of water for about
an hour and the stock is then strained off. The almonds are

pounded in a mortar and the hot stock is mixed with them.

The fried bird is then placed in a casserole with the onions and garlic. The hot stock and almond mixture is added to the frying pan, which is well scraped to detach the juices of the bird. This stock is then poured over the bird, etc, in the casserole or saucepan and the wine and salt are added. The casserole is covered and stewed for 3 hours.

The sauce is passed through a sieve before serving. The beaten yolk of an egg is added, it is heated slowly over a low fire, stirred all the time, and then poured over the bird.

PAVO ADOBADO (CASTILLA LA VIEJA)

MARINADED OR SOUSED TURKEY

a turkey of about 9 lb

FOR THE MARINADE:

3 *bayleaves*	1 *sliced onion*
3 *cloves garlic*	*salt*
4 *peppercorns*	*sufficient white wine to cover*

2 *sliced large onions*	4 *peppercorns*
2 *tomatoes*	2 *cloves*
6 *cloves garlic*	*salt*
½ *teaspoon cinnamon*	*oil*

The turkey is cleaned and disjointed and put into the marinade for four hours. It is then taken out and dried well.

Sufficient oil to cover the bottom is put in a large thick saucepan or casserole. The oil is heated and the turkey is added, together with all the other ingredients. The casserole is tightly covered and left to cook on a very low fire or in a slow oven for about $2\frac{1}{2}$ hours.

PARTRIDGE

De la perdiz lo que mira al cielo.
Del conejo lo que mira al suelo.
From the partridge—the breast.
From the rabbit—the hindlegs.

PERDICES FELIPE II (EL ESCORIAL)

PARTRIDGES PHILIP II

2 partridges

FOR THE STUFFING:

2 cloves of shallots, finely chopped
2 oz salchicha (sausage), finely chopped
1 oz smoked ham, finely chopped
24 grapes, stoned and peeled

The ingredients for the stuffing are all heated together, then the partridges are stuffed with the mixture and sewn. They are roasted in the oven for 12 minutes, then taken out and left to get cold. When cold they are covered with a good pastry and put in the oven for a further ten minutes. They are served on a piece of fried bread spread with foie gras. A thick Madeira Sauce is served with them.

From the Hotel San Lorenzo.

PERDICES A LA MESONERA (SEGOVIA)

PARTRIDGES À LA MESONERA

2 *lb whole small white French
  onions*
1 *lb chopped carrots*
1 *lb finely chopped Spanish
  onions*
¼ *lb salted ham*
¼ *lb butter*
½ *pint refined olive oil*
2 *oz flour*
2 *pints tomato sauce (freshly
  made)*

¼ *lb small new turnips, finely
  chopped*
2 *pints white wine*
1 *tumbler sherry*
6 *partridges*
2 *lb fried potatoes*
½ *teaspoon cinnamon*
2 *cloves*
a little chopped tarragon
salt and pepper

The partridges are floured and put in a large oven dish with
the seasoning, small onions, chopped onions, butter, carrots,
turnips, salted ham and oil and cooked in the oven for 30
minutes. Then the wine, sherry and tomato sauce are added
and it is allowed to cook for 1½ hours uncovered. If any of the
partridges are still tough a little stock is added and the cooking
continued.

The fried potatoes are served surrounding the partridges,
vegetables and sauce.

*For 6 people—though in England I think half this quantity would
suffice. From the Restaurant Mesón Candido.*

SALMOREJO DE PERDIZ A LA TOLEDANA (TOLEDO)

PARTRIDGE À LA TOLEDANA

This is like a baked custard of partridge surrounded by the breasts covered with a special sauce.

3 partridges are cleaned, a piece of fat bacon is tied on their breasts and they are roasted in the oven.

FOR THE SAUCE:

The hearts, livers, kidneys, gizzards and necks of the partridges are used. The roast partridges are removed from the oven. The excess fat is poured off, the leavings in the pan scraped and about 1 pint boiling water added. In this the giblets and neck are stewed. A dessertspoon of butter is placed in a saucepan with 1 teaspoon of finely chopped shallot, 2 tablespoons wine, 2 small slices of ham cut in pieces, and a bouquet of herbs. This is heated until boiling, stirring well, then ½ pint of the stock is added and 2 oz foie gras. It is again stirred well and seasoned.

The partridges are now placed in this, covered, and heated on a low fire for a few minutes to absorb the flavour. They are then taken out, drained and put aside. The sauce is kept at the side of the fire.

FOR THE MOULD:

The breasts and wings of the partridges are removed and put aside. The whole legs are cut off, the flesh taken off them and pounded down in a mortar, diluting with a little stock until a paste is formed.

FOR THE CUSTARD:

3 *eggs*
½ *pint partridge stock*

salt and pepper
a little grated nutmeg

The yolks of the eggs are well beaten with the paste, the stock added, and then seasoned with the salt, pepper and nutmeg. The stiffly beaten whites are folded in. This is then poured into a buttered soufflé case and stood in a tin of water in a moderate oven for about half an hour. It must not boil. When it is cooked it is removed and kept in a bain-marie until ready to serve.

It is turned out on a round dish. The partridge breasts are warmed in the sauce and then put on a plate round the mould and covered with a little sauce. The remaining sauce is served separately.

PERDIZ ESTOFADA (LOGROÑO)

PARTRIDGE STEW

1 *partridge*
1 *onion*
1 *head garlic, with a clove stuck*
  in one of the sections
1 *bayleaf*
1 *small tumbler oil*

1½ *tumblers red wine*
½ *tumbler wine vinegar*
salt
1 *dessertspoon chocolate*
½ *lb new potatoes or*
  1 *lb mushrooms, cooked apart*

Everything, with the exception of the chocolate, is placed in a saucepan and allowed to stew together. When cooked, the partridge is taken out and kept warm. The chocolate is mixed into the sauce and cooked for 2 minutes. The sauce is then strained and added again to the partridge. It is served with new potatoes or mushrooms.

From the Restaurante Adela.

PERDIZ EN CHOCOLATE (LOGROÑO)
PARTRIDGE IN CHOCOLATE

1 *partridge*	1 *breakfastcup boiling water*
1 *small chopped onion*	1 *tablespoon grated chocolate*
1 *tablespoon chopped parsley*	1 *tablespoon breadcrumbs*
2 *chopped cloves of garlic*	*oil and butter*
2 *tablespoons vinegar*	

The partridge is browned in a casserole on the fire in a mixture of oil and butter. Then the onion, parsley and garlic are added and, when browned, the vinegar and boiling water are poured in. This is then stewed slowly and, when cooked, the chocolate and breadcrumbs are stirred in and it is allowed to boil for some minutes.

PERDICES LO TORERO

PARTRIDGES À LA BULLFIGHTER

1 *partridge*
the heart, kidneys and liver of
  the partridge
4 *fillets of anchovies*
4 *thin rashers of fat bacon*
4 *tomatoes*

4 *green peppers*
1 *teaspoon chopped parsley*
salt and pepper
1 *glass white wine*
2 *thin slices raw ham, fried*

The heart, kidneys, liver, anchovies and bacon are all finely chopped, mixed together and seasoned.

The tomatoes and green peppers are seeded, peeled and slowly stewed together with salt, pepper, chopped parsley and a little water to prevent burning.

The partridge is stuffed with the giblets, etc, and then placed in an oiled oven dish with the mixed tomato and green pepper added.

The casserole is covered and cooked slowly for half an hour. Then the white wine is added and at the end of about another half hour it is served with the slices of fried ham.

PERDICES ESCABECHADAS

SOUSED PARTRIDGES

These are partridges soused as we souse herrings.

STAGE 1:

2 *partridges*	3 *cloves*
1 *tumbler oil*	2 *bayleaves*
½ *tumbler wine vinegar*	1 *teaspoon salt*
½ *tumbler white wine*	1 *onion*
1 *tumbler water*	1 *sprig parsley*
8 *cloves garlic*	1 *stick celery*
12 *peppercorns*	

STAGE 2:

¼ *pint wine vinegar*	*sufficient oil to cover completely*

The partridges are browned in the oven and then placed in a deep saucepan with all the ingredients required for stage 1. They are stewed in this mixture until they are tender. They are then drained well and dried.

They are now placed in the dish in which they are going to be preserved. The vinegar is poured over them and then sufficient oil to cover them completely. When cold the dish is covered and put in a cool place.

CODORNICES ASADAS

ROAST QUAILS

These are pot-roasted. They are placed in a pan with lard.
When browned, for each quail is added:

1 *glass stock*	*salt and pepper*
1 *wineglass white wine*	1 *bayleaf*
sprigs of parsley, marjoram and	*garlic*
thyme	

The pot is covered and the quails allowed to cook. When
cooked, the herbs and bayleaf are removed and the sauce
thickened with flour.

CODORNIZ CON TOMATE

QUAIL WITH TOMATO

The quails are cleaned and prepared. They are then seasoned
and in each quail is placed a little roll of fat bacon, ham and a
sprig of parsley. The quails are then fried in lard, turning and
browning evenly and they are removed, drained and kept in a
warm place.

For each quail 1 finely chopped clove of garlic and 1 finely
chopped tomato is fried in the same lard, stirring well until
there is a thick sauce, which is then seasoned. The sauce is
finally poured over the quails in an oven dish and they are reheated and served.

FAISAN AL MODO ALCANTARA
(ALCANTARA)

PHEASANT ALCANTARA

The pheasant is cleaned from in front, the breastbone is taken out and it is stuffed as follows:

Some duck livers are mixed with equal parts of butter, seasoned and passed through a sieve. To this is added a few large pieces of truffles which have been previously cooked in port wine. When the pheasant has been stuffed with this it is allowed to marinade for three days in port wine.

After this it is put in a saucepan, seasoned with salt and cooked in butter. When it is brown and practically cooked, the wine of the marinade is reduced and about 10 small truffles added; this is poured over the pheasant and allowed to cook for a further ten minutes. When this is finished it is served on a plate surrounded by the sauce and the truffles.

Partridge can be cooked in the same way.

H

PATO A LA SEVILLANA (SEVILLE)

DUCK À LA SEVILLANA

This is really best for wild duck such as a mallard.

2 *young mallards*
4 *cloves garlic*
oil for frying
salt and pepper
2 *large onions, sliced*
4 *tomatoes*
flour for coating
½ *tumbler medium sherry*
12 *olives, stoned*

2 *oranges, sliced*
1 *bayleaf*
1 *slice bread*
3 *red peppers*
1 *bouquet of herbs (i.e. bayleaf, parsley and thyme)*
1 *teaspoon chopped parsley*
1 *tumbler hot stock made with the giblets*

The dish takes a long time to do well and it is best started the day previously.

Two of the cloves of garlic are fried in the oil and then removed.

The duck are disjointed and lightly rolled in flour flavoured with salt and pepper. They are carefully browned in the oil and then removed. A large deep pan should be used and only some of the joints can be fried at one time. The duck are put in a colander to drain in a warm place.

The onions are now gently cooked in the same oil and when soft (they must not be brown) the tomatoes, which have been skinned, seeded and chopped, are added and the whole thing is allowed to simmer slowly.

When soft, the stock is added and the duck returned to the pan, which is now covered and allowed to simmer slowly for two hours, with the bouquet of herbs added.

The remaining garlic is chopped finely, the bread crumbled, 1 red pepper is chopped, and these are fried together in oil; then a little of the sauce from the cooking is mixed in and it is pounded in a mortar and added to the saucepan with the duck and seasoned with salt and pepper. The cooking is continued for a little longer and then the duck is again removed, care being taken to see that none of the onion, etc, adheres to it.

The sauce is now passed through a fine sieve, it is reheated, the sherry and duck are added and the pan is covered again for a few minutes. It should now be transferred to an open casserole in which it can be served. The olives are added, the sliced oranges are placed on the ducks and the dish put under the grill for about 5 minutes. The remaining peppers are baked, skinned, cut in strips, and arranged to decorate the dish.

PASTEL DE CONEJO (NAVARRE)

RABBIT PASTY

The rabbit is stewed and the bones removed. It is sprinkled with thyme and rosemary. A potato pastry is made, using oil. The rabbit is placed on half the pastry and moistened with the juice of the cooking. The other half is folded over and sealed and it is baked in the oven. Alternatively, small pasties can be made and fried.

The stock from the cooking of the rabbit is reduced and the pasty served covered with this as a sauce.

POTATO PASTRY:

1 *lb potatoes, baked in their skins, then peeled and sieved*
5 *oz flour*
½ *teaspoon baking powder*
½ *teaspoon salt*
½ *teacup oil*
1 *egg*

The egg is beaten with the oil. The potato and flour and salt
are mixed together and then gradually stirred into the egg and
oil. A workable mass should result, which can be rolled out
ready for use.

TORTA DE CONEJO (ALICANTE)

RABBIT TART

A rabbit of about 3 lb is cleaned and disjointed. A short pastry
case is made, using 1 lb flour, and baked blind.
  The rabbit is stewed with:

2 *chopped onions*	*salt*
2 *chopped tomatoes*	*sufficient water to cover*
2 *chopped red peppers*	

The rabbit and vegetables are then placed in the pastry case
and heated in the oven.

LEBRE ESTOFADA CON JUDIAS (CUENCA)

STEW OF HARE AND FRENCH BEANS

1 *medium-sized hare*	1 *sprig thyme*
1 *lb French beans*	½ *tumbler white wine*
1 *onion, chopped*	*salt and pepper*
2 *cloves garlic, chopped*	*oil for cooking*
1 *bayleaf*	1 *wineglass wine vinegar*
1 *chili*	

The hare is placed in the casserole with the oil, onion, garlic, bayleaf, thyme, white wine and vinegar. The casserole is covered and put in a slow oven until the hare begins to be tender. The French beans are prepared, boiled and drained, then added to the casserole, seasoned, and the dish cooked for a further 20 minutes. Just before serving a chili is cut into very small pieces and added.

EMPANADAS

⅓ *cup oil (in which a clove of*   1 *egg*
    garlic has been fried)   *salt*
⅓ *cup water*   *flour*
⅓ *cup melted butter*

The water, butter, oil and egg are beaten well together and flour is gradually added until a workable mass is produced. This is then rolled out on a floured board. It can either be cut in miniature pasties or in one large one.

The filling is made up of the remains of any chopped meat and vegetables, which must be moistened with a little liquid. The mixture is placed on one half of the pasty only, the edges are moistened all the way round and the top is folded over and the edges pressed together. It can then, as stated, either be fried in oil or can be painted with beaten egg and cooked in the oven.

If fish is used the classical mixture is slightly different. The pastry is prepared as follows:

⅗ *teacup oil*   1 *tablespoon white wine*
⅖ *teacup water*   1 *egg yolk*
1 *tablespoon orange juice*

The procedure is then as previously. Any remains of fish can be used, preferably moistened with a little Béchamel and chopped parsley added.

VEGETABLES

VEGETABLES

Comer verdura y echar mal ventura.
Eat greens and be healthy.

Vegetable dishes in Spain are often a course in themselves. Potatoes boiled or fried may be served with meat but, although there are many vegetables in a stew, they are rarely eaten as an accompaniment to meat. One does find them boiled, but, especially in the north, delicious plates of mixed vegetables are served.

The menestra is not as one might think, a soup, but a vegetable dish.

The simple recipes given here for vegetables to accompany meat, are put in a separate category from those which form a course by themselves.

ALCACHOFAS

ARTICHOKES

Only French artichokes are found in Spain. To prepare them the stalks are cut off and the outer leaves removed. The tops can then be cut off, but the correct method is to break each leaf separately where the colour changes from light to dark green. As the inner leaves are reached, less and less need be broken off. When the artichokes are large and old, only the heart can be used. When prepared, they should be well washed in salted water.

French artichokes can simply be boiled and served with

melted butter, or they can be used cold in salads (see Salads, page 273). The following is a pleasant way of cooking them:

6 *artichokes*	1 *chopped onion*
1 *oz chopped ham*	1 *dessertspoon flour*
1 *oz chorizo (garlic sausage)*	*oil for frying*

The artichokes are quartered and placed in boiling water to cover them, and left for about 5 minutes. They are then drained, placed in another pan of boiling water and seasoned. The change of water prevents them from being bitter. They are then taken out, drained and fried lightly in oil with the chopped ham and chorizo. They are removed and put in a clean pan. The onion is then fried in the same oil, the flour is stirred in and cooked a little and this is then poured over the artichokes and everything is reheated.

For 3 people.

ALCACHOFAS FRITAS

FRIED FRENCH ARTICHOKES

The outer leaves of the artichokes are removed and the hard tops of the remaining leaves are broken off. They are then quartered, dipped in beaten egg and fried in deep oil.

ACELGA

SILVER BEET (BEET-SPINACH)

In the south of Spain no spinach is grown, and this vegetable takes its place. It has a much larger, longer, tougher leaf than spinach and a long white fleshy stalk. Both leaf and stalk can be used, or, if wished, only the leaf. The stalks can be chopped off and cut in pieces about 1½–2 inches long. They are then boiled and served with vinaigrette or they can be dipped in egg and breadcrumbs and fried. The acelga whole or the leaves can be used for any dish for which spinach is used. Foreigners to Spain often cannot tell the difference from spinach.

ACELGA (MALAGA)

SILVER BEET

1 *bunch silver beet*
1 *clove garlic*
1 *teaspoon paprika*
½ *teacup breadcrumbs*
1 *sliced sweet red pepper, seeded*

1 *sprig parsley*
1 *dessertspoon vinegar*
salt
oil for frying

The silver beet is cooked like spinach and drained well. The garlic, paprika, crumbs, parsley and pepper are fried together in oil, then all pounded in a mortar. This is then mixed with the vinegar, salted, poured over the silver beet and served hot.

HABAS A LA ASTURIANA
(ASTURIAS)

BROAD BEANS À LA ASTURIANA

2 *lb broad beans*
½ *lb small potatoes, cut small*
¼ *lb young carrots, sliced*
¼ *lb onions, finely chopped*
2 *oz ham, finely chopped*

oil for frying
½ *pint stock*
½ *tumbler white wine*
½ *teaspoon paprika*
2 *cloves garlic*

Sufficient oil is used to cover the bottom of a deep saucepan. When hot the garlic and onions are added, allowed to brown slightly, and then the ham is stirred in. The pan is placed at the side of the fire and the paprika mixed with the contents of the pan. The pan is then replaced on the fire and the beans and carrots added with the wine and stock. This is then seasoned and, when it boils, the pan is covered and the vegetables allowed to cook very slowly for half an hour. The peeled potatoes are then added, the cooking is continued until the potatoes are soft, and the dish is then served.

HABAS A LA MONTAÑESA

BROAD BEANS À LA MONTAÑESA

2 *lb broad beans*
oil for cooking
2 *oz bacon cut in small pieces*
2 *oz chopped ham*
1 *onion*
2 *sweet red peppers*

1 *dessertspoon flour*
1 *dessertspoon sugar*
1 *dessertspoon chopped parsley*
½ *teaspoon chopped thyme*
salt and pepper

The bottom of a casserole is covered with oil and the bacon slowly cooked in it. When cooked, the ham and onion are added, the casserole is covered, and put on a very low fire for about half an hour. The peppers are then added, the flour is stirred in, and the beans, parsley and thyme added. The vegetables are seasoned, covered with the lid, and cooked on a very low fire until the beans are tender.

HABAS CATALANA (CATALUNIA)

CATALAN BROAD BEANS

3 lb broad beans
oil for frying
½ lb lean bacon
3 small onions, chopped
2 cloves garlic, chopped
½ lb tomatoes, peeled, seeded and
   chopped

salt and black pepper
grated nutmeg
a bouquet of herbs—bayleaf,
   mint, wild thyme (flgerola)
1 wineglass anis
1 wineglass peppermint
½ pint stock

The oil is heated in a saucepan and the bacon, onions and garlic heated in it and cooked a little. Then the tomatoes are added and cooked two or three minutes. The beans are now stirred in and seasoned with salt, black pepper and grated nutmeg. The bouquet of herbs, anis and peppermint are added and the hot stock stirred in. The pan is covered tightly with greased paper and the lid, and cooked for about an hour on a slow fire.

For 5 people.

JUDIAS VERDES A LA ESPAÑOLA

FRENCH BEANS À LA ESPANOLA

2 lb French beans
oil for frying
2 cloves garlic, chopped fine
1 tablespoon chopped parsley

3 red peppers, baked and skinned
and cut in thin strips
salt and pepper

The French beans are cooked in boiling salted water and then drained. The garlic and parsley are fried in the oil and the peppers added. When cooked, these are mixed with the beans and reheated.

ZANHORIAS

CARROTS

1 lb young carrots, scraped and
sliced
2 oz butter, or a little more
1 onion, finely chopped
1 tablespoon flour

1 pint milk
1 well-beaten egg yolk
salt and pepper
oil

The carrots are gently cooked in the butter, then removed and kept warm. The onion is placed in the oil and, when soft, the flour is stirred in and cooked a little. The boiling milk is added at the side of the fire, stirring vigorously all the time; it is then allowed to cook until thickened, when the carrots are added. Just before serving, the beaten yolk is stirred in and the seasoning added.

For 3–4 people.

COLIFLOR FRITA

FRIED CAULIFLOWER

The leaves and central stalks are discarded and only small sprigs of the cauliflower are used. These are left to marinade in salt, parsley and vinegar for about half an hour. They are then well drained, dipped in beaten egg, fried in hot oil, and carefully drained.

GUISANTES A LA BILBAINA (BILBAO)

PEAS À LA BILBAINA

1 *pint picked peas*
1 *finely chopped onion*
oil for frying
1 *lb small new potatoes, boiled*

1 *clove chopped garlic*
¼ *pint stock*
salt and pepper

The onion and peas are cooked in the oil and when half cooked the potatoes are added, then the hot stock, which is allowed to boil. Just before serving, the garlic is fried in a little oil and poured over the dish.

For 2–4 persons.

PEPPERS

The large red and green peppers, sometimes called paprikas in England, are called pimientos in Spain—'pimiento verde' when green and 'pimientos morrones' when red. Of these peppers there are two types: one with a blunt end and thick flesh, the other slightly smaller and thinner and funnel-shaped. They taste very similar and I can find no different names for them, but the larger kind is best used for stuffing and the smaller in stews and salads. The red powdered pepper obtained from these peppers and commonly known as paprika in England, is called pimenton—or, in Andalucia, pimiento colorado.

Capsicum is the Latin name for chili, used in Spain and sometimes in England too. The common name for chili in Spain is guindilla. The pepper made from this is the cayenne pepper called pimienta de cayena.

Both red peppers and chilis can be dried and kept for use out of season. Chilis can easily be crumbled between the fingers to make a crude powdered pepper. They can also be used fresh; and are used to flavour stews, rice dishes, etc.

Dried red peppers should be placed in cold water for a few minutes before using. They can also be used fresh or tinned. When fresh they are usually skinned and the stalks and seeds removed before cooking. To skin them, grill them until the skin becomes black and can be peeled off.

Green peppers are not usually skinned. The stalk and seeds are removed before cooking.

PATATAS EN AJO POLLO (MALAGA)

POTATOES IN AJO POLLO

2¼ lb potatoes
3 cloves garlic
1 small bayleaf
1 clove
pepper and salt

1 sprig parsley
1 slice bread
1 dessertspoon saffron
about ½ teacup oil for frying
6 almonds

The slice of bread is fried in the oil with the garlic, bayleaf, parsley and almonds. When fried they are all pounded together in a mortar with the saffron, and the oil which is left is poured over the peeled and sliced potatoes in a casserole at the side of the fire. The mixture in the mortar is moistened with a little cold water and then added to the potatoes in the casserole. These are then just covered with boiling water, the salt, pepper and clove are added and they are cooked until tender.

EL AJO DE LA MANO (JAEN)

'THE GARLIC OF THE HAND'

1 lb potatoes
2 dried red peppers
3 cloves garlic

paprika, salt
½ teaspoon vinegar
2 teaspoons oil

The potatoes are boiled with the peppers. They are then drained and sliced. The garlic is pounded in the mortar with the salt, paprika, oil and vinegar and is then mixed with the potatoes and reheated before serving.

PATATAS CASTELLANAS

CASTILIAN POTATOES

2 *lb potatoes*
1 *large onion*
1 *tablespoon flour*
1 *teaspoon red pepper (paprika)*

1 *clove garlic*
½ *bayleaf, crumbled*
½ *tumbler oil*
salt and pepper

The chopped onion and garlic are heated in the oil. When they begin to brown, the potatoes, cut in thick slices, and the red pepper are added. They are left to cook over a low fire, the pan being shaken from time to time, and when the potatoes begin to soften, the flour is mixed in. They are then covered with boiling water, seasoned, and the crumbled bayleaf is added. The saucepan is covered and the dish left to cook very slowly for one hour.

BATATAS (MALAGA)

YELLOW SWEET POTATOES

These can be served as a vegetable or a sweet or as jam. They can also be boiled like ordinary potatoes, baked in the oven or fried.

There is another kind of sweet potato, called moniatos, which is orange in colour and can be used in the same way as batatas.

TOMATOES

Tomatoes in Spain are usually better skinned and seeded before using for cooking, especially in the south. They are usually plucked before they are ripe; the seeds are very hard and there is always a large amount of fibrous tissue in the centre. Not everybody removes the seeds and some even omit to skin them. Cultivation is often poor in Spain and artificial means of replacing minerals in the soil are practically unknown. Hence the tomatoes are not so juicy and succulent as in many other countries.

Tomatoes are used largely in salads or sauces. The peasants stew tomatoes sliced with garlic and oil and chopped onion until a thick paste results, and this is used with meat, fish, etc, and is universal.

VEGETABLE DISHES SUITABLE FOR ENTRÉES

ALCACHOFAS RELLENAS

STUFFED FRENCH ARTICHOKES

The outer leaves and the hard tops of the artichokes are removed. They are then boiled in salted water.

6 *French artichokes*
2 *oz ham, finely chopped*

2 *oz veal or beef, previously*
   cooked

Each artichoke is chopped in half and the minced mixed meat and ham placed in the centre. They are then dipped in beaten egg and fried in oil. They are seasoned and served.

ESPARRAGOS AMAGUEROS (MALAGA)

WILD ASPARAGUS

1 *bundle asparagus*
1 *sweet red pepper*
1 *sprig parsley*
2 *cloves garlic*
4 *eggs*

½ *cup breadcrumbs*
oil for frying
salt
1 *dessertspoon vinegar*

The asparagus is boiled in salted water, drained and placed in a flat oven dish. All the other ingredients except the eggs are fried in the oil and then pounded in a mortar, the vinegar being added at the last minute; this mixture is poured over the asparagus. The eggs are then broken over the asparagus and the dish is heated in the oven until the eggs are set.

CAZUELA DE HABAS VERDES A LA GRANADINA

CASSEROLE OF BROAD BEANS À LA GRANADINA

2¼ *lb broad beans*
4 *onions, finely chopped*
2 *cloves garlic, finely chopped*
oil for frying
2 *tomatoes*
bouquet of herbs: bayleaf, parsley
   and mint

10 *very young French artichokes*
1 *teaspoon saffron*
½ *teaspoon cumin*
½ *teaspoon white pepper*
1 *slice fried bread*
6 *eggs*

The beans are shelled, put in a saucepan, covered with cold water and put on the fire. The onions and garlic are finely chopped and fried in the oil. When brown, the chopped tomatoes are added.

When par-boiled, the beans are drained and mixed with the tomato, etc, and enough boiling water is added to cover them. The bouquet of herbs and the whole artichokes are then added. The lid is placed on the saucepan and everything is cooked together until the beans are soft and very little liquid is left.

The saffron, seasoning, and the fried bread crushed into crumbs are then mixed well into the contents of the saucepan. The mixture is put in one large oven dish or several smaller dishes, the eggs are broken over it and the dish or dishes placed in the oven and heated until the eggs are cooked.

HABAS A LA RONDEÑA (MALAGA)

BROAD BEANS À LA RONDEÑA

2 *lb broad beans*
¼ *lb smoked ham*
4 *hard-boiled eggs*
1 *sweet red pepper, finely chopped*

2 *tomatoes, finely chopped*
1 *onion, finely chopped*
oil for frying

The beans are par-boiled and drained. The tomatoes, red pepper, onion and ham—which has been cut in small pieces—are fried in the oil. The beans are stirred in, then the hard-boiled eggs are finely chopped and sprinkled over the dish, which is reheated. Alternatively, raw eggs can be used, two for each person, and these are then broken over the beans and the dish is heated in the oven until the eggs are cooked. Individual dishes can be used if desired.

PATATAS Y JUDIAS VERDES A LA EXTREMADURA (EXTREMADURA)

POTATOES AND GREEN BEANS À LA EXTREMADURA

2 *lb potatoes*
2 *lb beans*
1 *large onion, chopped*
2 *tomatoes*
2 *green peppers*

oil
salt and pepper
5 *cloves garlic, chopped*
1 *bayleaf*
2 *tablespoons chopped parsley*

The potatoes are peeled and coarsely sliced. The French beans are prepared as usual. The tomatoes are peeled and cut in squares. The green peppers are roasted and peeled and cut in rings. Sufficient oil is used to cover the bottom of a deep sauce-pan, then everything is put in at once and seasoned. The pan is tightly covered and it is cooked very slowly for an hour.

CALABACINES RELLENOS

STUFFED COURGETTES (BABY MARROWS)

6 *courgettes*	1 *tablespoon butter or oil*
2 *lb tomatoes*	1 *pint béchamel sauce*
1 *chopped onion*	2 *tablespoons grated cheese*
1 *clove garlic*	*salt, pepper and sugar*

The courgettes are peeled and halved lengthways. The pulp is carefully removed. They are then cooked for about 10 minutes in boiling salted water.

The chopped onion and garlic are fried slowly. When soft, add the peeled tomatoes, from which the seeds have been removed, salt and pepper and a little sugar. Cook very gently in a covered pan for about 10 minutes. Then place the cooked marrows filled with the stuffing in an oiled fireproof dish.

Make one pint of béchamel sauce and add the grated cheese. Pour this over the stuffed courgettes. Sprinkle them with more cheese and a few dabs of butter and cook in a moderate oven for 15–20 minutes until the top has browned slightly. Serve in the same dish.

Instead of cheese, two beaten eggs may be added to the béchamel when it is cooked, and again poured over the courgettes and baked in the oven.

An alternative stuffing can be made with:

1 *chopped onion*
6 *tomatoes, peeled and seeded*
½ *teacup crumbs moistened with milk*
2 *tablespoons remains of meat or fish*

1 *teaspoon chopped parsley*
1 *teaspoon chopped marjoram*
salt and pepper
yolk of 1 egg
oil for frying

Cook the onions and tomatoes as before. Then add the other ingredients, stir well and cook for another 5 minutes. Take off the fire and add the egg yolk. Fill the courgettes, heaping the stuffing up. Dab butter on top and cook for 5 minutes. Serve with béchamel sauce for fish and tomato sauce for meat.

JUDIAS ENCARNADAS A LA MADRILEÑA (MADRID)

RED BEANS À LA MADRILEÑA

1 *lb dried red beans (previously soaked)*
2 *oz bacon in thin slices*
2 *oz chorizo, sliced*
1 *tablespoon flour*

1 *finely chopped onion*
1 *clove garlic, finely chopped*
paprika, pepper and salt
1 *wineglass oil*

The beans are just covered with water in a saucepan and brought slowly to the boil, together with the bacon and chorizo. They are then simmered slowly until tender. The chopped garlic and onion are fried gently in the oil. When they begin to brown, the flour is mixed in. Some of the hot liquid of the beans is then added and stirred in well. This is then mixed in the pan with the beans, seasoning is added, the pan is allowed to simmer for another five minutes and the dish is then ready for serving.

MENESTRA DE GUISANTES

PEA STEW

1 *breakfastcup of peas*
2 *oz butter*
1 *oz chopped ham*
left-over pieces of chicken or game
2 *green artichokes, chopped (the heart and tender leaves only)*

1 *dessertspoon chopped parsley*
salt
1 *chopped clove of garlic*
pepper
water to cover
flour

The butter is melted in a saucepan and the ham and peas heated in it. The chicken and green artichokes are then added and allowed to get hot, then boiling water, sufficient to cover, is added. It is brought to the boil, seasoned with salt, and the parsley, garlic and pepper added. The pan is covered and the contents are simmered until the vegetables are cooked.

The flour is then gradually stirred in, and still stirring, is allowed to cook until it thickens. The dish is then served.

Sufficient for 2 people.

CACHELES (LA CORUÑA, GALICIA)

2 *lb potatoes*
1 *small green cabbage*
2 *oz ham*
2 *oz chorizo (garlic sausage)*

oil for frying
1 *oz bacon*
½ *teaspoon red pepper*
3 *cloves garlic*

The potatoes are peeled and boiled and then left to drain. The cabbage is boiled in a saucepan with the chorizo and ham. When it is cooked the cabbage is taken out and drained.

The bacon is chopped fine and fried in the oil with the chopped garlic and red pepper. The potato and chopped cabbage are mixed in with this. The ham and chorizo are then served as one dish and the potato and cabbage, etc, as another.

BERENJENA RELLENA

STUFFED EGGPLANT

4 *eggplants*
½ *lb mushrooms*
1 *tablespoon grated cheese*

salt and red pepper (paprika)
1 *beaten egg*
breadcrumbs

Remove the stalk and leaves from the eggplant. Cut in half and remove the seeds. Cook in boiling salted water until partially cooked. Remove and drain.

Fry the mushrooms, drain and chop finely. Mix with the grated cheese, salt, red pepper and the beaten egg.

Put the eggplants on a buttered fireproof dish and spoon the mixture into them. Sprinkle crumbs on the surface, dab with fat and bake in the oven.

FABADA ASTURIANA (OVIEDO)

This is a famous dish made from dried white haricot beans.

1 *lb dried white beans, soaked*
overnight
¼ *lb bacon (salted cured pork)*
1 *pig's ear (substitute a piece*
of ham)
½ *lb morcilla Asturiana (blood*
sausage)

1 *oz longaniza (pork sausage)*
1 *oz salted beef*
½ *lb lean bacon*
1½ *pints water*
2 *oz lard*
salt and pepper
1 *teaspoon saffron*

The beans are placed in a saucepan with the cold water on a moderate fire and, when simmering, all the other ingredients—except the lard and the saffron—are added. The dish is covered and is cooked on a low fire or in the oven for three hours. After 1½ hours the lard, which has been melted and mixed with the saffron, is gradually diluted with a little of the liquid of the saucepan and then poured into the stew. The cooking is continued until the beans are completely tender.

CHICHAROS (ZARAGOZA)

PEA CAKES

These are sweet cakes made of dried peas, which must be previously soaked.

1 *lb peas*
1½ *lb flour*
½ *lb sugar*
4 *eggs*

1 *oz butter*
grated peel of 1 *lemon*
pinch of salt

The peas must be chopped fine. The flour is placed in a mixing bowl, a well is made in the centre with every other ingredient in it and they are gradually mixed in. Little cakes about 1 inch in diameter are made from this mixture and are baked in the oven.

PIMIENTOS RELLENOS (LOGROÑO)

STUFFED PEPPERS

6 *medium-sized sweet red peppers*	½ *pint stock*
1 *teaspoon flour*	1 *bayleaf*
oil for frying	1 *tumbler tomato sauce*
1 *beaten egg and flour for coating*	*salt and pepper*

FOR THE STUFFING:

½ *lb good fillet, finely minced*	1 *beaten egg*
1 *clove chopped garlic*	½ *cup breadcrumbs*
1 *sprig chopped parsley*	*salt and pepper*

The fillet is finely chopped and mixed with the parsley, breadcrumbs, garlic and seasoning. The beaten egg is then added. The red peppers, which have had their stalks and seeds removed, are then baked slightly in the oven. They are stuffed, placed in a deep pan in hot oil, fried gently, then removed.

The flour is then mixed in and allowed to cook, and the chopped parsley, garlic and hot stock are added. This is then passed through a sieve and seasoned.

The pimientos are now placed in a casserole, the sauce poured over them, the bayleaf is added, the casserole covered and the peppers are gently simmered for a quarter of an hour, stirring from time to time. After half an hour's cooking the tomato sauce is added.

From the Restaurante Adela.

PIMIENTOS VERDES RELLENOS

STUFFED GREEN PEPPERS

4 *sweet green peppers*   6 *teaspoons Worcester sauce*
3 *cloves garlic chopped*   3 *beaten eggs*
2 *teaspoons mixed herbs*   2 *breakfastcups tomato sauce*
4 *teaspoons butter or oil*

Mix all dry ingredients, add Worcester sauce and beaten egg. Melt the fat and fry this mixture in it slowly.

To make the tomato sauce cook 2 tablespoons chopped onion in oil without browning. When soft add 1 lb tomatoes, quartered, a bouquet of herbs and seasoning. Allow to simmer until soft. Pass through a sieve and make up to one pint with hot stock or water.

Cut the peppers in half lengthways, remove stalks and seeds and wash well. Partially cook in boiling salted water. Drain and dry and fill with the mixture, then put them in a greased oven dish. Pour the tomato sauce over them and cook for about 20 minutes in a slow oven.

PIMIENTOS RELLENOS CON MAÑOS DE CERDOS (OVIEDO)

GREEN PEPPERS STUFFED WITH PIG'S TROTTERS

Allow 2 pig's trotters for 2 fairly large green peppers. The trotters are boiled until the meat is falling off the bones. The skin and bones are then removed, the pieces of flesh are drained, dried and fried in lard. The peppers have the stalks and seeds removed and are stuffed with the meat seasoned with pepper and salt, and baked.

PISTO (LA MANCHA)

This is the Spanish version of the Provençal Ratatouille.

1 *lb small marrows (courgettes)*	½ *teacup oil*
1 *lb tomatoes, skinned, seeded and chopped*	2 *cloves finely chopped garlic*
	1 *teaspoon chopped parsley*
1 *lb sweet red peppers, sliced*	*salt and pepper*
½ *lb onions, finely chopped*	

The oil is heated in a saucepan and the onion, garlic and parsley gently cooked in it. The red peppers are then added, the pan is covered and put on a very low fire for about ten minutes. The courgettes are peeled and quartered. If very young it is not necessary to remove the seeds, but if older the seeds and fibrous strands must be removed. The tomatoes and courgettes are then added, cooked very slowly for half an hour and seasoned.

I

QUINAD (IBIZA)

This is a vegetable stew which is eaten in Ibiza on Good Friday. The recipe was given to me by an Ibizenco. Quinad is not a Spanish word and the spelling is as near as I can get it. There is a green plant growing wild on the island which they call verdura (simply green vegetable). This is mixed with the leaves of bleda (silver beet) and guisias (wild white peas). They are boiled for a few minutes in a large quantity of water, which is then thrown away. The vegetables are then covered with fresh water, a little oil, and seasoned.

TORTA DE ACELGA

SILVER BEET (BEET-SPINACH) TART

This is good eaten hot or cold. Spinach can be substituted for silver beet.

1 *bundle of silver beet*	1 *chopped hard-boiled egg*
(see page 235)	1 *beaten egg*
1 *chopped tomato*	3 *oz grated cheese*
2 *onions (1 chopped)*	*salt and pepper*
2 *cloves garlic (1 chopped)*	1 *slice bread*
1 *chopped sweet red pepper*	*oil for frying*

A pastry case is made with $\frac{1}{2}$ lb flour and $\frac{1}{4}$ lb butter, or it can be rolled out and shaped like a large Cornish pasty. If a case is made there must be sufficient left to cover the contents of the tart.

The silver beet is well washed and is placed in boiling water seasoned with salt in which one onion and 1 clove of garlic have been par-boiled. The onion and clove of garlic are left in the pan whilst the silver beet is cooking. When cooked, it is well drained, and the silver beet, onion and garlic are placed in a large sieve and the water squeezed out by pressing down with a plate. It is now removed and finely chopped.

The slice of bread is fried in the oil with the chopped onion, garlic, tomato and red pepper. When fried, everything is taken out of the pan and ground down in a mortar and the oil is added.

The chopped egg and cheese are mixed with the silver beet and this is added to the contents of the mortar, together with salt and pepper. The beaten egg is then mixed in. This is placed on half the thinly rolled pasty and the rest is folded over. It is painted with milk or white of egg and baked in the oven.

MENESTRA DE ACELGA

A DISH OF SILVER BEET (BEET-SPINACH)

2 bundles of silver beet (see page 235), par-boiled, well drained and without stalks

FOR THE FILLING:

1 *large onion, finely chopped*	3 *chopped hard-boiled eggs*
2 *oz ham, finely chopped*	1 *raw egg*
1 *dessertspoon chopped parsley*	*salt and pepper*
the chopped stalks of the silver	*a little stock to moisten*
beet	*oil for frying*

All ingredients except the raw egg are fried together in a little oil, then moistened with the stock and reheated. The mixture is seasoned with salt and pepper and a raw egg is beaten into it.

The leaves of the silver beet are stuffed with this mixture, folding them over like a parcel and tying them up with cotton. They are then dipped in egg and flour and fried. They are drained, the cotton removed, and they are put on the serving dish. A good tomato sauce is then poured over them.

FRITO DE ESPINACAS Y COLLEJAS (GRANADA)

FRIED SPINACH AND YOUNG CABBAGE

1 *bunch spinach (approximately*   *pepper and salt*
   2 *lb)*   6 *eggs*
2 *small cabbages*   1 *beaten egg*
oil and butter for frying   *breadcrumbs*
4 *spring onions, sliced*

The spinach and cabbages are boiled in salted water, drained and chopped. The onions are chopped and cooked in equal quantities of oil and butter. The greens are then added and seasoned with salt and pepper. The beaten eggs are added and a large omelette made and allowed to cool. This is then cut into circles with a small pastry cutter. These small tortillas are then dipped in egg and breadcrumbs, fried until a golden brown, and served immediately.

MENESTRA DE ESPINACA

A DISH OF SPINACH AND EGGS

2 *bundles spinach (about 4 lb)* 2 *oz ham cut in eight equal*
1 *oz lard*   *pieces*
2 *oz chopped ham*   4 *hard-boiled eggs*

The spinach is boiled in plenty of salted water, drained and chopped. The chopped ham is fried in the lard, then drained and mixed with the spinach. Eight little nests are formed with the spinach and chopped ham, and in each is placed a square of ham and half a hard-boiled egg. A little red pepper is sprinkled on the egg and it is ready to serve.

JUDIAS A LO TIO LUCAS

A VEGETABLE STEW

2 *lb haricot beans (soaked in salt*   1 *sprig parsley*
  water for some hours)   1 *sprig thyme*
1 *head garlic*   *salt and pepper*
1 *bayleaf*   2 *tablespoons oil*
6 *peppercorns*   1 *pint water*
2 *cloves*

The garlic is browned in the oil and removed. The beans are then added with the crumbled bayleaf, the peppercorns, cloves and herbs and allowed to cook slowly, stirring from time to time to prevent burning. The boiling water is added and the cooking is continued until the vegetables are tender. A little chopped ham or chorizo may also be added.

OLLA CORDOBESA (CORDOBA)

STEW OF CORDOVA

2¼ *lb chick-peas*
½ *lb tocino*
  (*fat bacon*)

1 *white cabbage of about* 1 *lb,*
  chopped
1 *quart boiling water*

The chick-peas are soaked for at least 12 hours and drained. Boiling water is poured on them, they are left in this water for about 5 minutes and then drained. They are put in a pan with the quart of boiling salted water and, after simmering for an hour, the piece of fat bacon is added. After simmering for another ½ hour the cabbage is added and it is again simmered for half an hour. The stew is then ready for serving.

    The chick-peas available in England usually take rather more than 2 hours to cook. Sometimes as long as 5 hours.

GUISADO DE TRIGO (ALBACETE, LA MANCHA)

STEW OF INDIAN CORN

6 *corn cobs*
½ *lb chick-peas, soaked overnight*
1 *pig's foot*
¼ *tumbler oil*
2 *chopped tomatoes*

2 *sweet red peppers, sliced*
2 *onions, finely chopped*
2 *cloves garlic, chopped*
salt and pepper
1 *teaspoon mint*

The Indian corn has the outer leaves, etc, removed and is placed in a deep saucepan of boiling water, together with the pig's foot and chick-peas. The water should only just cover them, they are allowed to boil vigorously and then more cold water is added until the grains of the corn burst open. It is then simmered until the chick-peas are tender, and most of the water is absorbed. The tomatoes, peppers, onion and garlic are simmered in the oil until they form a thick sauce. This is then mixed with the stew which is seasoned and allowed to cook slowly for another 5 minutes. Just before serving it is sprinkled with the chopped mint.

MENESTRA DE LEGUMBRES FRESCAS (MURCIA)

A VEGETABLE AND EGG DISH

4 *eggs*
2 *spring onions, chopped*
1 *carrot, chopped*
1 *globe artichoke, quartered*
½ *cup shelled peas*
1 *sprig celery, chopped*
1 *small turnip, chopped*
½ *small cauliflower (the flowers only)*
2 *sliced potatoes*

¼ *lb haricot beans*
2 *tomatoes, without seeds or skin, chopped*
¼ *lb ham, cut in small squares*
1 *tablespoon flour*
1 *bunch asparagus*
½ *pint stock*
seasoning
about half a cup oil for frying

The ham and all the vegetables—with the exception of the tomatoes and the asparagus—are allowed to simmer in the oil for about 15 minutes. The tomatoes are then stirred in and simmered for a few minutes. The flour is then mixed in and allowed to cook for a few minutes, then the stock is added and the seasoning. The pan is covered and left to cook slowly for about 10 minutes.

The vegetables are then placed on a dish and decorated with the asparagus previously boiled and the poached eggs.

TUMBET MALLORQUIN (MALLORCA)

2 lb potatoes, sliced
2 lb eggplant, sliced but not peeled
2 lb green peppers, sliced

2 lb tomatoes, skinned and seeded and made into a sauce (see Tomato Sauce)
3 cloves garlic

The vegetables are all fried separately in oil and drained. They are then placed in layers in an oven dish and seasoned. The tomato sauce is poured over them and they are sprinkled with biscuit crumbs. They are then placed in a hot oven for 15 minutes.

From the Restaurante Orientes, Ca'n Tomeu, Palma.

FIDEOS A LA CATALUÑA

SPAGHETTI À LA CATALUÑA

1 lb spaghetti
½ lb lean pork, chopped
¼ lb salchicha, sliced
2 onions, chopped
4 large tomatoes, skinned, seeded and chopped
2 oz fat bacon, chopped

2 finely chopped cloves of garlic
12 hazel-nuts
12 pine-nuts
red pepper
1 tablespoon grated cheese
¼ teaspoon saffron
1 pint stock

The bacon and pork are placed in a casserole and cooked slowly until brown, then the onions are added, together with the garlic and tomatoes. When cooked, it is seasoned with salt and pepper. The hot stock is now added with the sliced salchichas, and it is brought to the boil and simmered for ten minutes. The spaghetti is then added.

The nuts and saffron are pounded in a mortar and mixed with a little of the liquid from the casserole and then stirred in. It is cooked until the spaghetti is tender (about 7 minutes). The grated cheese is sprinkled over it and it is heated for 2–3 minutes in the oven. More grated cheese can be served separately.

FIDEOS A LA MALAGUEÑA I (MALAGA)

SPAGHETTI À LA MALAGUEÑA I

2¼ *lb cockles*	1 *bayleaf*
1 *chopped onion*	½ *lb spaghetti*
2 *sliced sweet green peppers*	1 *teaspoon saffron*
2 *cloves garlic, chopped*	*salt and pepper*
3 *tomatoes, peeled and seeded*	*oil for frying*

The cockles are well cleaned, boiled and shelled, the water in which they have cooked being reserved.

The onions, peppers, tomatoes, and bayleaf are fried in oil, and the salt, pepper and saffron added.

The water from the cockles is allowed to boil until only ½ pint is left and it is then gradually stirred into the tomato mixture. The spaghetti is boiled, placed in a dish and mixed with the cockles, and the sauce is poured over it.

FIDEOS A LA MALAGUEÑA II (MALAGA)

SPAGHETTI À LA MALAGUEÑA II

This is another spaghetti dish from Malaga.

2¼ *lb fresh anchovies*
½ *lb potatoes*
4 *sweet red peppers*
1 *breakfastcup cooked shelled peas*

2 *chopped cloves of garlic*
½ *lb spaghetti*
salt and pepper

The spaghetti is cooked, then tossed in oil. The anchovies are fried, 4 or 5 together forming a fan by pressing their tails together.

The potatoes and red peppers are cut in small squares and fried separately, and then mixed with the peas and spaghetti. The fans of anchovies decorate the spaghetti.

FRITAS

FRITTERS

This is a good dish for an informal supper.

4 *oz chicken, minced together with*
4 *oz ham*
1 *tablespoon flour*

salt
1 *breakfastcup milk*
2 *oz butter*

A roux is made with the flour and butter. The milk is added and stirred in well at the side of the fire. The ham and chicken are then cooked slowly in this and seasoned with salt. When a fairly solid paste is formed it is made into sandwiches cut from stale bread and firmly pressed together. These are painted with beaten egg, sprinkled with breadcrumbs and fried in very hot oil.

GACHAS MANCHEGAS (LA MANCHA)

oil for frying	*paprika*
1 *lb pig's chap cut in small pieces*	1 *clove*
2 *oz almorta flour (made from the*	1 *teaspoon caraway seeds*
beans of the vetch)	*pepper*

The pig's chap is fried slowly in the oil and then removed. To the oil and the resulting fat the spices and then the flour are added and mixed in well. Half a pint of boiling water is then added and the mixture is stirred and allowed to simmer until thickened. This sauce is then served with the bits of pig's chap on top.

MIGAS I

'LITTLE BREADCRUMBS'

In the dishes styled *Migas*, small squares of bread are usually soaked in milk and then fried with or without the accompaniment of small pieces of meat, etc. The origin of this dish is mediaeval or earlier.

MIGAS II (ANDALUCIA)

BREADCRUMBS

½ *lb brown bread without the*
   crust, cut in small squares
½ *teaspoon salt*
oil for frying

6 *cloves garlic*
½ *teaspoon paprika*
small pieces of chopped ham or
   fillet of veal

The bread is sprinkled with the salt and sufficient water just to moisten it. It is well mixed and then left for 24 hours in a cool place.

The next day the cloves of garlic are fried in the oil and removed when brown. The paprika and squares of bread are then fried in the oil, the bread being turned continuously so that it is evenly browned. Small squares of ham or veal can be fried with the squares and in Jaén squares of chopped chorizo (garlic sausage) are added.

MIGAS III (ARAGON)

BREADCRUMBS

In Aragon the migas are moistened with water, sprinkled with salt and left in a serviette overnight. They are then fried in oil which has had garlic fried in it. These are then served with tomato sauce or small squares of ham can be fried with them. Strangely enough they can also serve as a sweet and are eaten with chocolate or with grapes. The origin of this dish is probably Celtic.

EL PAN DE COSTRA AL AJO
(MALAGA)

TOASTED BREAD AND GARLIC

This can be eaten at any meal. For each slice of bread one needs:

2 or 3 *cloves garlic*	*salt and pepper*
1 *dried red pepper*	1 *dessertspoon oil*
juice of half a Seville orange	

The garlic is pounded in a mortar with the red pepper, salt and pepper. The juice of the orange is stirred in and then the oil. The mixture is then spread on the slice of bread, which is heated in the oven before serving.

In Estepona this is known as 'Gazpacho Colorado'.

MIGAS DE CARLOS IV

½ *lb bread cut in ¼-inch cubes*	¼ *lb fat bacon cut in ¼-inch cubes*
½ *teaspoon salt*	¼ *lb chorizo of Extremadura*
milk to moisten	*(garlic sausage) cut in ¼-inch*
oil for frying	*cubes*
6 *cloves garlic*	½ *lb grapes, peeled and seeded*

The bread cubes are moistened with milk, sprinkled with salt, wrapped in a cloth and left for a few hours.

The cloves of garlic are fried in oil and removed when brown. The cubed bacon and chorizo are then placed in the pan and, when fried, the bread is added. The bread must be turned constantly to brown evenly and not allowed to get too hot. All the oil must be absorbed when the bread is cooked.

The cubes, together with the bacon and chorizo, are placed on a dish, the grapes are placed on top of them, heated in the oven, and served hot.

SALADS

Con la ensalada, vino o nada.
With salad, wine or nothing.

Salad in Spain usually means lettuce with a dressing of oil and vinegar, but others, such as tomato sliced with a French dressing and chopped parsley, or tinned red peppers, may be ordered. The following recipes are for some of the other varieties served in Spain.

ENSALADA DE ALCACHOFAS

SALAD OF GREEN ARTICHOKES

The artichokes are boiled, the hard green part of the leaves and all the outer leaves are removed. The heart and tender leaves are cooled and covered with a vinaigrette. A few slices of hard-boiled egg can be mixed in with them.

ENSALADILLA HOTEL ESPAÑA PARA ENTREMESES (MADRID)

SALAD HOTEL ESPAÑA FOR HORS-D'ŒUVRE

Chopped tinned red peppers are mixed with chopped pickled salmon or bonito and chopped prawns. This is mixed with mayonnaise and decorated with slices of hard-boiled egg.

From the Hotel España, Guadalajara.

273

ENSALADA DE PIMIENTOS

SALAD OF RED OR GREEN PEPPERS

6 *sweet peppers*
4 *small tomatoes*
2 *small onions*

1 *teacup of vinaigrette*
parsley

Grill the peppers on the fire, turning carefully, and when the
skin blackens peel them. Remove the stalks and seeds, cut in
half lengthways and then slice finely. Skin and remove the seeds
from the tomatoes and chop the onions. Mix with the vinaigrette and sprinkle with parsley.

PIPIRRANA JAENERA CON JAMON
SERRANO (JAEN)

JAEN SALAD WITH HAM SAUCE

2¼ *lb tomatoes*
3 *sweet green peppers*
4 *hard-boiled eggs*
½ *lb tinned bonito or soused*
   tunny fish
4 *cloves garlic*

1 *dessertspoon oil*
1 *slice bread without the crust*
½ *teaspoon salt*
1 *tablespoon vinegar*
Serrano ham

The tomatoes are peeled, seeded and chopped. The peppers are
grilled, peeled and chopped with the whites of the eggs.
   The cloves of garlic are pounded with the yolks, a dessertspoon of oil and the bread which has been soaked in water.
When this has been well mixed, the salt and vinegar are added.

In summer this is iced and served with slices of dried Spanish ham.

ENSALADA DE SAN ISIDRO (MADRID)

This is a salad of lettuce with pickled tunny fish. Tunny fish is pickled or soused in Spain as are herrings in England. Tinned tunny is a good substitute.

ENSALADA DE SEVILLA

SALAD OF SEVILLE

Endive chopped with stoned olives, dressed with vinaigrette, sprinkled with tarragon.

SAUCES

SAUCES

The most commonly used sauce in Spain is the tomato sauce. Béchamel, Sauce Tartare and Sauce Espagnole are also well known, but the last two are only served in the bigger restaurants. The recipes given in this chapter are for local sauces, little known outside Spain.

ALI-OLI

15 *cloves garlic*   *juice of* ¼ *lemon*
1 *pint olive oil*   2 *egg yolks*
salt

The garlic is crushed in a mortar and the oil gradually beaten in until a thick heavy paste is formed; the egg yolks are then beaten in and more oil added. When all the oil is used up, the lemon juice and salt are added.

This sauce is used to accompany meat or fish dishes. In Alicante it is served with grilled rabbit or rabbit tart.

SALSA DE ALMENDRAS CON YEMA

ALMOND SAUCE WITH YOLK OF EGG

½ *lb almonds*
3 *hard-boiled egg yolks*

a little milk or oil

This sauce is used for fish. The almonds are skinned and baked in the oven. They are then pounded to a paste in a mortar with the yolks. They are diluted with a little milk or oil and sprinkled on fish before serving.

SALSA DE ALMENDRAS

ALMOND SAUCE

yolks of 2 hard-boiled eggs
6 toasted almonds
1 teaspoon chopped parsley

salt and pepper
1 pint milk

The egg yolks, almonds and parsley are pounded together in a mortar and salt and pepper added. To this is added the milk, and it is allowed to simmer over a low fire until reduced by half. Pass through a sieve and serve.

SALSA PARA AVES

SAUCE FOR BIRDS

¼ *lb butter*   4 *egg yolks, well beaten*
¼ *lb flour*   *salt for seasoning*
½ *tumbler white wine*

The butter is melted and the flour cooked in it until it bubbles and begins to go yellow. On the side of the fire the wine is added and beaten in well and then, still at the side of the fire, the beaten eggs are gradually stirred in. The sauce is seasoned and poured over the birds when they are served.

SALSA A LA MADRILEÑA (MADRID)

A SAUCE FOR CHICKEN

The legs, neck, heart, lungs, liver and kidneys of a chicken are cooked in 4 pints water to make stock. This should be seasoned and cooked for several hours as ultimately there should only be 1 pint of stock. The chicken is roasted and when cooked is skinned and carved, the skin being added to the stock.

An onion is finely chopped and fried in oil in a saucepan with a teaspoon of chopped parsley, a crumbled bayleaf and a teaspoon of wild marjoram. The boiling stock is added and the sauce simmered for half an hour. It is then strained and poured over the chicken.

SALSA PARA FIESTA DE NATIVIDAD
(IBIZA)

A CHRISTMAS SAUCE

This curious recipe was given me by a 'local' in Ibiza. It is a great treat for the country people at Christmas and is used as a hot drink after eating.

6 eggs
½ lb almonds, dried in the oven and
    then ground down in a mortar
2 pints chicken stock

a few sprigs of saffron
3 tablespoons sugar
1 teacup dry biscuit crumbs
1 teaspoon cinnamon

The saffron, sugar, biscuit crumbs and cinnamon are all ground together in a mortar and a little chicken stock added. Everything is now mixed together and the hot stock gradually stirred in. Six eggs are well beaten and added to the pan at the side of the fire, stirring vigorously with a wooden spoon and always in the same direction, until the sauce has thickened.

SALSA VERDE

GREEN SAUCE

4 tablespoons parsley
1 cup oil

salt and pepper

The parsley is ground down in a mortar until it is like a thick paste. The oil is beaten in drop by drop. It is then seasoned.

SALSA DE NUECES PARA CARNE DE CERDO

NUT SAUCE FOR PORK

1 *breakfastcup shelled walnuts*   1 *pint milk*

The nuts should be skinned and then ground down in a mortar. They are mixed with the milk and boiled until the milk is reduced to half a pint. To skin walnuts, pour boiling water over them and rub off the skin when cool enough to handle.

SALSA DE PATATAS (JAEN)

POTATO SAUCE

This potato sauce is served mainly with fish dishes.

½ *lb potatoes*   1 *bayleaf*
2 *tablespoons oil*   1 *clove*
2 *tomatoes*   1 *pint boiling water*
1 *red pepper*   *salt*
2 *cloves garlic*

All the vegetables are chopped finely and allowed to cook slowly in the oil. When soft, the boiling water, salt and clove are added and the sauce is simmered for about 5 minutes, stirring well all the time. It is then passed through a sieve, reheated, skimmed and served with the fish.

SALSA DE TOMATE

TOMATO SAUCE

1 *large chopped onion*
1 *clove garlic*
8 *tomatoes, chopped*

½ *tumbler oil*
seasoning
1 *chopped red pepper (optional)*

The onion and garlic are very slowly stewed in the oil. The tomatoes are added and they are left to simmer until the sauce thickens. They are then seasoned and can be used as an addition to a dish or as a sauce in which to reheat certain foods.

The refined version is to skin and seed the tomatoes. If liked, a chopped red pepper can also be cooked with the tomatoes.

Quantities are optional, and in practice rather less than half a tumbler of olive oil is preferred.

SALSA AMARILLA

YELLOW SAUCE

6 *hard-boiled eggs*
2 *tablespoons Madeira*
2 *tablespoons oil*
salt

½ *tumbler clarified stock*
1 *tablespoon vinegar*
½ *teaspoon mustard powder*
½ *teaspoon white pepper*

The egg whites are passed through a fine sieve. The yolks are mixed with the Madeira, then the oil is beaten in drop by drop. The sauce is seasoned with salt, the stock and vinegar stirred in, then the mustard and pepper, lastly the whites.

DESSERTS AND SWEETS

DESSERTS AND SWEETS

Mejor quedar con gana que estar enfermo mañana.
Better to remain hungry than to be ill on the morrow.

••

In Spain a meal is almost invariably finished with fruit. The bigger hotels and restaurants may also offer ice cream in the summer. Caramel Cream, called 'flan', is the one common sweet in the south, whilst in the north one is offered the inevitable 'yemas', little sweets made with yolks of eggs, sugar, etc. Tinned peaches are the alternative: they are one of the best brands of tinned peaches in the world and retain the flavour of the peach. Turron, the soft or hard Spanish nougat, may be taken with coffee. Cheese can be obtained if asked for but is not usually on the menu.

Little cakes and biscuits are found all over Spain in great variety. They are eaten at any time of the day with coffee. The 'mantecados' and 'polvorones', which are very dry, more like biscuits than cakes, are sometimes eaten with sherry. Some of these cakes and sweets are served on special occasions, for example, 'Hueso de Santos' (Saint's bones), which are eaten on All Saints' Day.

A few recipes for biscuits, cakes, yemas, etc, are given, together with a few of the less common desserts, which are usually only found in private houses.

TORRIJAS

white bread   *butter*
milk   *honey*
beaten egg

Small pieces of white bread without the crust are cut into squares of about 3 inches by 2 inches. They are soaked in milk and then drained. They are dipped in beaten egg and fried in butter. They are then put in a buttered oven dish, covered with a mixture of equal parts of honey and water and allowed to cook slowly in the oven.

ROSCON DE BONIATOS

DESSERT OF SWEET POTATOES

4 *large sweet potatoes*   *sweet syrup*
3 *eggs*   *cinnamon*
2 *tablespoons ground almonds*

The potatoes are baked in the oven and, when cooked, are skinned and sieved. They are then mixed with the yolks of the beaten eggs and the almonds. The resultant mass is placed in a buttered fire-proof dish in the form of a ring and the syrup (heated to make it run freely) is painted over it. The whites of the eggs are stiffly beaten with one tablespoon of sugar and placed on top. Cinnamon is then sprinkled on them, the dish is placed in a moderate oven and cooked for 15–20 minutes until the meringue is slightly browned. It can be served hot or cold but is better cold.

DULCE DE LECHE

MILK SWEET

10 *egg yolks*
4 *tablespoons flour*
1 *pint milk*

$\frac{1}{2}$ *teaspoon grated lemon peel*
$\frac{1}{2}$ *lb sugar*

Whip the eggs with the sugar and the flour and grated peel. Heat the milk and mix with the yolks, then return to the fire and heat until it thickens like a custard. Pour it into a greased tin or dish about 2 inches deep. When cold cut into fingers. Dip in beaten white of egg, roll in grated bread and fry in butter. Sprinkle with sugar and serve.

For 6 persons.

LECHE FRITA (VALENCIA)

FRIED MILK

First a custard is made with 3 eggs, 1 pint of milk and 3 table-spoons of flour. This must be cooked until it has well thickened. It is then poured into a tin to cool. Small pieces of this are then floured, dipped in egg and fried in oil. They are powdered with sugar and served.

K

CUAJADA (VALENCIA)

JUNKET

This is simply a junket made from milk turned with rennet, and mixed with sugar.

BOLLO MAIMON (CASTILLA LA VIEJA)

Bollo Maimon and Arroz con Leche are served on feast days. The Bollo Maimon is made from a biscuit mixture which is shaped in the form of the bull-ring. It is also served at wedding feasts.

ARROZ CON LECHE (CASTILLA LA VIEJA)

MILK AND RICE

½ *lb rice*   6 *dessertspoons sugar*
2 *pints milk*   *grated rind of* 1 *lemon*

The rice is placed in a saucepan, covered with cold water and cooked on a hot fire for five minutes. It is strained and washed in cold running water. Then it is returned to the saucepan. The milk and the lemon rind are allowed to come to the boil very slowly, then strained and poured over the rice. This is allowed to simmer for another ten minutes. Four dessertspoons of sugar are then stirred in and the rice is cooked slowly for another 20 minutes or until it is soft and has absorbed the milk. It is then poured into a dish and allowed to cool. When cold, the remaining sugar is sprinkled over it, it is browned under the grill and then served.

MANZANAS FRITAS

FRIED APPLES

2 *lb apples*
4 *tablespoons sugar*
1 *teaspoon cinnamon*

2 *tablespoons flour*
½ *tumbler beer*
1 *tumbler cognac*

The apples are peeled, cored and sliced horizontally. They are then sprinkled with half the sugar, the cognac is poured over them and they are left to soak overnight.

The cinnamon, remaining sugar and flour are mixed together and the beer is gradually added. The apples are then coated in this mixture and fried in butter.

TORTERA SEVILLE

TART

This is a special sweet tart eaten at Christmas. It is a sweet pastry which is filled with 'cabello de angel' (see page 15) and cooked in the oven.

BISCUITS

PASTAS DE ALMENDRAS MALLORQUINAS (MALLORCA)

ALMOND BISCUITS

½ lb almonds   2 egg whites
½ lb sugar

The almonds are skinned and toasted in the oven and all
except 12 are then minced or crushed in a mortar. The sugar
and almonds are mixed together. The eggs are well beaten and
then folded in. The mixture is dropped, a teaspoonful at a time,
on an oiled tin. There should be enough to make a dozen
biscuits. An almond is placed on the centre of each and they
are baked in the oven for 20 minutes.

MANTECADOS

½ lb pork lard   2 tablespoons sugar
1 wineglass rum or white wine   flour

The lard, wine or rum, and sugar are well mixed together and
flour is gradually added until a firm mass results. It is formed
into small circles about 1 inch in diameter and ½ inch thick.
They are baked in a hot oven and then powdered with sugar.

MANTECADOS DE ASTORGA (LEON)

BISCUITS OF ASTORGA

½ *lb butter*   ½ *lb flour*
½ *lb icing sugar*   ½ *teaspoon cinnamon*
6 *eggs*

The sugar and butter are creamed and the eggs are beaten in one by one. The flour and cinnamon, mixed together, are then gradually stirred in. A dessertspoon of the mixture is placed in little paper cases and then cooked in a moderate oven for ten minutes.

ALMENDRADOS (CASTELLON)

These are a variety of mantecados.

2 *dessertspoons sugar*   1 *teaspoon cinnamon*
2 *dessertspoons powdered almonds*   *grated rind of* 1 *lemon*
2 *egg whites*

The whites of eggs are beaten well, gradually mixing in almonds, sugar, cinnamon and lemon peel. Teaspoons of the mixture are then dropped on a buttered tin and cooked in a moderate oven for 10 to 15 minutes.

TORTAS DE ACEITE (SEVILLA)

OIL BISCUITS

½ *lb flour*   1 *glass dry anis*
¼ *lb sugar*   *rind of* 1 *lemon, grated*
2 *tablespoons oil*   ½ *teaspoon salt*
1 *egg*

The flour, sugar, salt and grated lemon peel are mixed together.
A well is made in the middle and the beaten egg, oil and anis
are poured into it and gradually mixed in with the flour, etc.
The mass is then rolled out thinly and cut into small circles
which are cooked in a hot oven for about 10 minutes.

PERRUÑAS (CORDOBA)

BISCUITS

½ *lb pork lard*   5 *tablespoons sugar*
1 *lb flour*   ½ *teaspoon cinnamon*
2 *egg yolks*   *grated skin of* 1 *lemon*
1 *egg*

The sugar and fat are beaten together until creamy, then the
beaten yolks and the egg are added and lastly the flour, cinnamon and lemon peel, which have been previously mixed together. When well mixed, small flat oval biscuits about the
length of an egg are formed. They are then dipped in beaten
white of egg, powdered with sugar and cooked in a hot oven.
These rise and swell a good deal, so leave a good space in
between each.

L

POLVORONES (ANTEQUERA)

BISCUITS

1 *lb flour*
½ *lb pork lard*
½ *lb sugar*

1 *wineglass dry anis*
1 *dessertspoon cinnamon*
icing sugar to cover

The sugar and fat are creamed and the cinnamon mixed with
the flour. The anis is gradually added to the sugar and fat, then
the flour is worked in with the hands. It is then rolled out to
about ½ inch in thickness and cut into small ovals. They are
cooked in a hot oven for about 10 minutes, then rolled in icing
sugar and wrapped in paper.

ROSCOS

RINGS

½ *lb flour*
2 *eggs*
2 *dessertspoons milk*
2 *oz butter*

2 *oz almonds, skinned and*
    finely chopped
¼ *lb sugar*
a pinch of salt

The butter and sugar are creamed together, the beaten yolks
and one beaten white mixed in, then the milk. The flour is
gradually added until it forms a mass which can be easily rolled
out. It is rolled out in a square about half an inch thick, then
folded over twice, making another square. It is re-rolled and
folded three times, then rolled out again and cut into small
rings. The remaining white of egg is well beaten, each ring

dipped in it, and the almonds sprinkled on them. They are then baked for 10 minutes in a hot oven.

ROSQUILLOS DE ALMAJARO (LA MANCHA)

LITTLE SPIRALS OF ALMAJARO

2 eggs
the juice of 1 lemon
enough oil to fill 1 egg shell
flour

oil for frying
icing sugar to sprinkle on them
  when cooked

The eggs are beaten with the oil and the lemon juice is mixed in. Then the flour is added and worked in well. It is then rolled out and cut into small pieces and shaped into spirals about 3 inches in diameter. The oil is heated, and when it reaches smoking point the fire is turned very low and the little spirals are fried. They are then drained and rolled in the icing sugar.

ROSQUILLAS DE SAN ISIDRO (MADRID)

4 eggs
$\frac{1}{4}$ lb sugar
$\frac{1}{2}$ lb flour
1 wineglass anis del mono
  (see page 46)

$\frac{1}{2}$ teaspoon baking powder
1 teaspoon of the seeds of anis,
  roasted in the oven and crushed
  in a mortar

The eggs and sugar are well beaten over warm water. The oil and anis del mono and aniseed are added, and finally the sifted flour and baking powder are folded in. About 12 little balls are then formed and a hole is made in the middle of each. They are placed on a greased tin, painted with beaten egg and cooked in a hot oven.

CAKES, BREAD, TARTS, ETC

BIZCOCHOS BORRACHOS
(GUADALAJARA, CASTILLA LA NUEVA)

'DRUNKEN CAKES'

12 *egg yolks*
12 *egg whites, well beaten*
9 *tablespoons sugar*
1 *lb flour*

$1\frac{1}{2}$ *lb sugar heated to the point of*
caramelization and mixed with
$\frac{1}{2}$ *pint Malaga wine*
powdered cinnamon

The egg yolks are beaten with the sugar, then the flour is gradually mixed in. The well-beaten whites are folded in and the mixture put in small greased cake tins. These should only be half filled, and are put into a hot oven for about 10 minutes.

When cooked, they are taken out of the cases and allowed to cool. Meanwhile the syrup of sugar and Malaga is prepared and poured on to the cakes, which are then sprinkled with powdered cinnamon.

BIZCOCHOS

SPONGE CAKE

3 *eggs*
3 *dessertspoons sugar*

grated rind of 1 *lemon*
3 *dessertspoons flour*

The yolks are beaten separately with the sugar and the lemon rind. The stiffly beaten whites are folded in, then the flour. It is then cooked in a tin in a hot oven.

BUÑUELOS CLÀSICOS

These are the classical buñuelos which one can see being fried at any Spanish fair. They are circular rings, light and good to eat in the early hours of the morning at the Seville fair.

2 oz yeast
1 pint warm water
1 lb flour

¼ lb sugar
oil for frying

The yeast is mixed with the water and the flour is added gradually, being well and continuously beaten by hand. It is left in a cool place, covered with a cloth, until it has risen to double its original size. The circles are formed by hand, an extremely difficult operation for the uninitiated, whereas the fair people make them easily and quickly. They are flung into the boiling oil and swell up enormously. They are then drained, sprinkled with sugar and eaten hot.

BUÑUELOS DE VIENTO (MADRID)

A form of choux paste made with lard. They are eaten on All Saints' Day.

½ lb flour
¼ lb pork lard
1 teacup water
1 teacup milk
1 dessertspoon sugar

½ teaspoon salt
6 eggs
grated rind of 1 lemon
1 dessertspoon cognac

The milk, water, cognac, lard, salt and sugar are all melted together, and when they come to the boil the pan is placed on the side of the fire and the flour, mixed with the grated lemon rind, is beaten in. The pan is then returned to the fire, and the contents beaten until a thick mass, which clings to the spoon, is formed. The saucepan is then placed at the side of the fire and the eggs are beaten in one by one. Teaspoons of this mixture are fried in deep hot oil. When cold they are split and filled with cream, or simply served coated with sugar.

CANTELO (ASTURIAS)

This is a special bread baked in a ring form, which is broken into small pieces and given to the guests by the bride and groom at their wedding, with an accompanying glass of wine.

CHURROS I

Churros are the traditional breakfast dish of Spain. Usually the maid rushes out and buys them piping hot for breakfast, at which time one drinks thick chocolate and a glass of milk. They are also cooked at all fairs and are good to eat hot in the small hours.

Literally yards of churros cook at a time in great cauldrons of boiling oil. On a large scale, the breakfast churros are made with a vast 'churrero', a glorified icing syringe, which holds about 3–4 pints of the churro mixture at a time and which a man holds strapped to his shoulder. One can make them at home. Here is a simple recipe:

deep oil for frying
5 oz flour
1 pinch salt

½ teaspoon bicarbonate of soda
¼ pint water

The salt, flour and bicarbonate of soda are mixed together and then gradually mixed with the water. The oil must be smoking in the deep frying pan. The churros are made by allowing the mixture to fall from an icing syringe with a wide bore into the hot oil in the form of a continuous spiral, starting in the centre and widening out to the periphery of the pan. This is not at all an easy operation, although it looks simple in the hands of an expert. It must be done quickly and evenly and the churros picked out, drained on paper and sprinkled with sugar. They are broken into the required lengths.

CHURROS II

Here is another recipe for making churros for coffee-time.

1 pint water
½ teaspoon salt
1 lb flour

oil for frying
sugar
1½ oz butter

This is cooked like a choux paste. The butter is melted in the water and the pan is placed at the side of the fire and the flour is mixed in, together with the salt, stirring all the time; it is cooked until the mass is solid and leaves the pan. It is then fried in deep oil. One can pull it out and roll it in one's hands in long lengths of about ½ inch in diameter but it is best made with an icing syringe. The churros, when cooked, are rolled in sugar and are ready for use.

CORTADILLOS RELLENOS DE SIDRA (ANDALUCIA)

PUMPKIN PASTIES

This means literally 'short lengths filled with pumpkin'.

1 *small pumpkin*
sugar
cinnamon
oil for frying

bread dough made with:
1 lb flour, ½ oz yeast, about
6 oz water (sufficient to make
a dough)

The bread dough is made and left to rise. Meanwhile take a small pumpkin and bake it in a moderate oven for about half an hour. When soft, remove the skin and pips and mash with ½ lb sugar to 1 lb pumpkin and ¼ teaspoon cinnamon.

The dough is then rolled out very fine and is cut in squares rather like ravioli is cut. On half the square a little of the pumpkin mixture is placed, and the other half is folded over and the edges well sealed together. These are then fried in oil.

FLAN DE PASCUAS (IBIZA)

TART FOR EASTER FROM IBIZA

A good pastry is made, using ½ lb flour, ¼ lb butter and 1 egg. Line a pastry tin with it and fill it as follows:

Thin slices of cheese, which is made from a mixture of goat's and sheep's milk, are placed in the bottom of the case. This is then sprinkled with sugar and six eggs are broken one by one on top of the cheese and again sprinkled with sugar. One egg is then beaten with about 2 tablespoons of chopped mint and poured over the eggs. Some more sprigs of mint are laid on top and the flan is baked in the oven.

GLORIAS

These are little pastries filled with sweet potatoes and almonds.

1 *lb sweet potatoes*	$\frac{1}{4}$ *lb flour (approx.)*
$\frac{1}{4}$ *lb sugar*	$\frac{1}{4}$ *lb icing sugar*
$\frac{1}{4}$ *lb ground almonds*	6 *dessertspoons oil*
6 *dessertspoons aguardiente*	1 *teaspoon cinnamon*
(*dry anis*)	*rind of* 1 *lemon, grated*
$\frac{1}{2}$ *glass white rum*	

The sweet potatoes are cooked in their skins in the oven and then peeled and sieved. The purée is reheated with the sugar in a saucepan for a few minutes and the almonds and cinnamon then mixed in. This mixture is put on one side to cool. The aguardiente, rum, oil and lemon peel are mixed with the flour until a firm paste is formed, which is then rolled out very finely. Small circles of about 3 inches in diameter are cut out of the mass. The filling is placed on half and they are then folded over in half-moon shapes, painted with white of egg and cooked for 15 minutes in a hot oven. They are then sprinkled with icing sugar.

HUESOS DE SANTO (GRANADA)
'SAINTS' BONES'

These should be eaten on All Saints' Day.

THE DOUGH:	½ lb potatoes
1 lb sugar	½ pint water
1 lb ground almonds	grated peel of 1 lemon

THE FILLING:	¼ lb sugar
6 egg yolks	1 tablespoon water

| icing sugar | lemon juice |

The potatoes are boiled in their skins, then peeled and mashed or passed through a sieve.

The sugar and water for the dough, and the grated lemon peel, are boiled together in a saucepan, being well stirred until thick. Then the ground almonds are mixed in, and lastly the purée of potatoes. This mixture is allowed to cool and then rolled out on a board to a fine paste, which is cut into strips about 3 inches by 2 inches. These are rolled round a skewer and cooked on a dish in the oven. In the country a sugar cane is often used instead of a skewer.

When cooked they are removed from the skewer and allowed to cool. The filling is then introduced into the central cavity, and they are iced with ordinary icing, flavoured with lemon juice.

The filling. The sugar is dissolved in the water in a saucepan, heated well, and then the yolks are stirred in. It is then stirred over the fire until thick and creamy, and allowed to cool.

MAGDALENAS

MADELEINES

12 *egg whites, whipped*   ½ *breakfastcup oil*
6 *whole eggs*   2 *lb flour*
1 *lb sugar*

Beat the sugar and oil together, then beat in the whole eggs and then the whites. Add the flour gradually, beating well until it is of dropping consistency. Put in buttered cake moulds and bake in a hot oven for about 12 minutes. This is the Spanish version of the French Madeleines.

PASTELES DE ALMENDRAS (VALENCIA)

NUT PASTIES

½ *lb flour*   1 *egg*
¼ *lb butter*   *water to bind*
½ *teaspoon salt*   *oil for frying*

A shortcrust pastry is made with the above ingredients, then shaped like a Cornish pasty, with the following filling:

½ *lb powdered almonds*   *sufficient water to bind to a*
½ *lb sugar*   *paste*

The pasty is then fried in oil instead of being baked in the oven.

PISTIÑES ANDALUCES (ANDALUCIA)

SOFT ANIS AND HONEY BISCUITS

3 tablespoons oil
rind of 1 lemon
1 wineglass white wine
1 teaspoon aniseed
½ lb flour

1 teacup honey to which is added
3 tablespoons water
oil for frying
icing sugar

The oil is placed in the frying pan and the entire lemon rind slowly fried in it. When the rind is tender the pan is put at the side of the fire and the aniseed added. When cool the lemon peel is removed and the oil strained and mixed with the wine and flour. The paste is rolled out a little less than ¼ inch thick, then cut into squares about 2 inches long. These are fried in oil and drained. The honey is boiled with the water and allowed to simmer. The pistiñes are placed in this syrup for a few minutes, then drained. They are then covered with icing sugar.

ROSCON

A CAKE IN THE FORM OF A RING

1 lb ground almonds
½ lb sugar
6 beaten egg yolks
½ teaspoon cinnamon

½ grated rind of 1 lemon
7 egg whites (6 beaten stiffly)
syrup made of 2 tablespoons sugar
and 4 of water

The ground almonds are mixed with the sugar, grated lemon peel and cinnamon, then the beaten yolks are gradually worked in. The 6 beaten whites are folded into the mixture, which is placed in a buttered ring mould. This is then cooked in a moderate oven. When cooked, the cake is tinned out, the syrup is painted over the cake and the remaining white of egg is beaten slightly and painted on top of it. It is returned to the oven for 2 or 3 minutes. This can be eaten hot or cold.

BIZCOCHO DE SAN LORENZO

SAINT LAURENCE'S CAKE

½ *lb skinned chestnuts*
½ *lb sugar*
6 *eggs*
6 *oz cornflour*

butter
½ *lb jar of jam*
1 *tablespoon orange flower water*
½ *pint milk*

The chestnuts are cooked slowly in the milk until tender and then sieved. The sugar and eggs are well beaten in a pan over hot water for 15 minutes and then the orange flower water is added. The sieved chestnuts mixed with the cornflour are gradually folded in. The cake is cooked in the oven in a buttered tin which should stand in another tin of water. When cooked it is cut in thick slices and covered with jam.

PAN DULCE

SPANISH SWEET BREAD

6 *eggs*
8 *tablespoons sugar*
6 *tablespoons flour*

1 *tablespoon stoned raisins*
1 *tablespoon candied peel*

Beat the yolks with the sugar, fold in the beaten whites and then the flour and fruit and beat well. Pour into a buttered tin and cook in a moderate oven.

SEQUILLOS

3 egg whites   rind of 1 lemon
½ lb sugar   20 roasted hazel-nuts

The whites and sugar are beaten together and the grated lemon peel and nuts added. The mass is separated into small ovals which are baked in a hot oven.

SUSPIROS (VALENCIA)

SIGHS

½ pint milk   1 dessertspoon sugar
¼ lb butter   ½ lb flour
grated rind of 1 lemon   6 eggs
¼ teaspoon salt   oil for frying

The milk, butter, salt and sugar are beaten together over the fire, stirring well all the time. When boiling, the flour is mixed in and stirred vigorously. When a smooth paste is formed it is put at the side of the fire to cool slightly. The eggs are stirred in one by one. Some oil is heated in a deep frying pan and pieces of the paste, about the size of a nut, are dropped into the hot oil. When cooked they are removed, drained well, powdered with sugar and cinnamon, and served.

TORTA DE BURZAGO (LEON)

In León there is a special tart for Easter which is filled with milk mixed with powdered dried chestnuts.

TORTERA DE SIDRA (SEVILLA)

TART OF SIDRA (A KIND OF PUMPKIN GOURD)

This is a special sweet for Christmas. It is a sweet pastry which is filled with 'cabello de angel' (see page 15) and cooked in the oven.

GACHAS (CADIZ)

This is rather an extraordinary sweet dish which resembles porridge.

3 *tablespoons oil*	2 *tablespoons flour*
1 *teaspoon seeds of anis*	½ *pint boiling water*

The aniseed is fried in the oil for about 15 minutes. The oil is then strained into a clean pan and the flour added, stirring all the time until it bubbles but does not brown. Now add the boiling water, beat well and allow to simmer until it thickens to the consistency of baked custard. This is then eaten with sugar, milk, honey, etc.

ALMENDRAS GARRAPIÑADOS
(CASTILLA LA VIEJA, ALBA DE TORRES)

TOFFEED ALMONDS

almonds   *cinnamon*
sugar

The almonds are skinned and dried, then placed in a saucepan
with a little water, a stick of cinnamon and double their weight
of sugar. They are stirred constantly until the sugar thickens
and bubbles. They are then left on the side of the fire and, when
they are cool, the process is repeated until the sugar is brown.

BATATAS CONFITADAS (MALAGA)

SWEET POTATOES

This is the confection made from sweet potatoes. They are
baked in their skins, peeled, cut in cubes, dipped in a thick
syrup and allowed to cool. The children love them.

TURRON I

NOUGAT

Turrón usually appears at fair-time. That of Jijona is soft,
whilst that of Alicante is like hard nougat with lumps of nuts
in it. It is sold in wooden boxes, or wrapped in greaseproof
paper. Some of this nougat is exported. It can be eaten with

coffee as dessert or is excellent eaten with milk cheese. Here is an easy recipe.

2 lb powdered almonds   *12 egg yolks beaten slightly*
2 lb sugar

The yolks are added to the almonds and sugar and beaten well until a paste is formed. This is then placed in a tin, covered with a cloth and weights left on it for 2–3 days. It is then ready for use.

TURRON II

SOFT SPANISH NOUGAT

1 lb ground almonds   *6 beaten egg yolks*
1 lb sugar   *1 beaten egg white*

The sugar and almonds are mixed together and the beaten yolks gradually added. Then the mixture must again be well beaten. The beaten white is then added.

Line a shallow oblong cake tin with greased paper, leaving sufficient paper to cover the top of the mixture when it is in the tin. Press down firmly and leave for 2 or 3 days with a heavy weight on top.

YEMAS

Yemas mean literally 'yolks', and recipes are many and varied, the main ingredients being sugar and eggs, i.e. fondants. Here is the recipe made with potatoes, and the children love it.

1 *lb sugar*   1 *lb cooked peeled potatoes*
1 *lb ground almonds*   3 *whole eggs*

The potatoes are passed through a sieve. The eggs are beaten
with the sugar and then mixed with the potatoes and almonds.
The mass is then formed into little round balls, coated with
icing sugar and left to dry in the air. Twenty-four hours later
they are wrapped in paper and are ready for use.

YEMAS VARIADAS

12 *egg yolks*   *almonds, dates, prunes, walnuts,*
½ *lb sugar*   *preserved cherries, etc, as required*

The yolks are beaten with the sugar in a double boiler until a
mass is formed. This is poured on to a slab previously
powdered with sugar, and the mass made into a long thin
sausage. From this small balls are made. These balls can be
used in any of the following ways:

Marked on one side with a hot iron to form a caramel.
Mixed with small pieces of crystallized cherry or angelica or
fruits.
Small pieces can be inserted into stoned dates or prunes.
Rolled round toasted nuts or almonds.

A syrup is made by beating ½ lb of sugar, 6 tablespoons of
water and a pinch of cream of tartar, stirring all the time and
skimming when it boils. It should boil until when dropped in
cold water it forms a soft white mass.
The yemas are then dipped in the syrup and placed on an
oiled slab. When cold they can be put in paper cases or wrapped
in fine paper.

YEMAS DE SANTA TERESA
(AVILA, PROVINCIA DE MADRID)

6 *egg yolks*
4 *dessertspoons sugar*
1 *tablespoon water*

½ *teaspoon powdered cinnamon*
1 *teaspoon grated lemon peel*

A thick syrup is made with the water, sugar, cinnamon and lemon peel, heating it slowly until the sugar is dissolved and then to the point of caramelization.

It is then mixed quickly with the beaten egg yolks in a saucepan on a low fire, beating vigorously with a wooden spoon until it is completely amalgamated. It is then left at the side of the fire and allowed to cool, the beating being continued. When it has thickened it is put on to a dish and allowed to get completely cold. When cold it is formed into a very long roll about 1 inch in diameter. It is coated with sugar, cut into equal pieces and shaped with the fingers into small balls.

A FEW DRINKS

VINO QUEMADO (ARAGON)

BURNT WINE

This is drunk in Aragon on Christmas Eve. It is red wine heated and flavoured with cinnamon, orange peel and sugar. In fact a variety of mulled claret.

TO DRINK WITH CALDERETE ASTURIANA

1 *bottle light sherry*	1 *litre water*
1 *bottle white wine* (*Prionata*)	3 *lumps sugar*
1 *bottle champagne*	*the rind of* 2 *lemons*

This is mixed together and left on ice for some hours. It is then ready for use.

SANGRIA

This is a form of red wine cup which varies considerably from one place to the next. It is an excellent drink for hot summer days. Any red wine can be used and the fruit varies with different houses.

1 *bottle red wine*	½ *lemon*
6 *cubes of ice*	6 *peaches cut in slices*
rind of one cucumber	1 *tablespoon sugar*

All ingredients except the ice are mixed together and the wine left in a cold place for an hour or more. The ice cubes are added just before serving.

PONCHE I

PUNCH

3 *egg yolks*   1 *wineglass cognac*
3 *dessertspoons sugar*   2 *stiffly beaten egg whites*

The yolks and sugar are beaten together then the cognac is
added and lastly the egg whites.

PONCHE II

PUNCH

3 *egg yolks*   1 *wineglass cognac*
3 *dessertspoons sugar*   1 *pint milk*

The yolks are beaten with the sugar, the cognac is stirred in
and then the very hot milk.

LINOYADA (LIMOYA-EZEN-BAYA) (BASQUE)

LEMONADE

the skin of 6 lemons   1 *pint white wine*
1 *pint water*   ½ *lb sugar*
1 *pint red wine*

The rinds are left in this mixture surrounded by ice for 24 hours
before serving, stirring from time to time to dissolve the sugar.

INDEX